PARENTING
Guide to
Positive Discipline

PARENTING

Guide to Positive Discipline

by Paula Spencer
with the editors of
PARENTING magazine

BALLANTINE BOOKS
NEW YORK

For George

A Ballantine Book
The Ballantine Publishing Group

Copyright © 2001 by PARENTING magazine

Illustration credits (by page number)
 ii Brad Wilson/Photonica
  2 Charles Thatcher/Tony Stone Images
 30 Stephen Derr/The Image Bank
 44 Barnaby Hall/Tony Stone Images
 60 Britt Erlanson/The Image Bank
 76 Jerome Tisne/Tony Stone Images
 98 Photonica

www.ballantinebooks.com

LIBRARY OF CONGRESS CATALOGING-IN-PUBLICATION DATA
Spencer, Paula.
    Parenting guide to positive discipline / by Paula Spencer with the editors of Parenting magazine.
        p. cm.
    Includes index.
    ISBN 0-345-41183-8
    1. Discipline of children. I. Parenting (San Francisco, Calif.) II. Title.

HQ770.4 .S64 2001
649'.64—dc21   2001025469

Text design by Michaelis/Carpelis Design Associates, Inc.
Cover photo ©Norbert Schäfer/Corbis Stock Market

Manufactured in the United States of America

First Edition: August 2001

10 9 8 7 6 5 4 3 2 1

Contents

CHAPTER 1
Why All Kids Need It   2

Laying the Groundwork Now
- Definition: Discipline ● Definition: Punishment

The Goals of Healthy Discipline
- Checklist: Rethinking Discipline

Why Kids Misbehave

The Eight Essential Elements
- Checklist: What Can You Expect at Different Ages? ● Checklist: Some Rules About Rules
- Checklist: Smart Routines Every Household Needs

Is My Child Spoiled?
- Hot Topic: Developing Responsibility
- Checklist: Chores for Beginners

CHAPTER 2
What's Your Discipline Style?   30

Which Shoe Fits?
- Checklist: Parents' Top Discipline Mistakes

When Parents Disagree
- Checklist: Whatever Your Style May Be . . .
- What We Do: "Our Parenting Styles Clash"

Contents

Contents

Foreword

Once upon a time, before I was a mom, I was sure that when I had kids they'd be wonderfully behaved and cooperative—with their friends, each other, and, of course, Mom and Dad. As a parent, I'd learn all the right things to say and do, so discipline would hardly be necessary.

Then I became a parent, and reality hit. My children, Jack and Laura, are wonderful. They've also been spirited, curious, and very age-appropriate. Which means that they've required discipline—loving limits to give them the space they've needed to flourish, feel confident, and get along well with others.

Are time-outs the most effective way to rein in a toddler? When do you try to negotiate, or give in? What's too strict? There are plenty of theories about discipline. Your mom, friend, neighbor, and pediatrician may each have a different opinion and favorite method.

But there's no one discipline rule that fits all kids and their families. So whom should you trust? Yourself. You know your child's temperament, and your own, better than anyone—whether you're coaxing your preschooler to get ready for bed, or in the throes of yet another of a toddler's *no*'s.

PARENTING *Guide to Positive Discipline* offers reality-tested information and insights to help you fashion the discipline styles that work best for you, whatever the stage or situation. It's a resource we hope you'll turn to for years.

Janet Chan,
Editor in Chief
PARENTING

Acknowledgments

Thanks to the following people for helping to produce this book: at PARENTING magazine, Bruce Raskin, Janet Chan, Lisa Bain, and Maura Rhodes. For reporting all of the family profiles, I'd like to thank Heidi Kotansky. For photo research, Caren Alpert. For additional research, Valerie Fahey. This book could not have been written without the thoughtful advice of the many families and parenting experts I've interviewed for PARENTING magazine over the years, especially Dr. William Sears, Dr. Marianne Neifert, Burton White, Lynda Madison, Peter Williamson, and James Windell. Finally, special thanks to my family for giving me the time to write this (as well as very relevant firsthand knowledge!): George, Henry, Eleanor, Margaret, and Page.

Introduction

*F*orget that I'm the author of a book about disciplining young children. As a mother of four, I'll be the first to admit that this is one aspect of parenting that is truly easier in theory than in practice. Discipline is hard. Discipline is endless. Discipline is tricky—something both invisible and quite obvious. And not least, discipline can cause even a patient, confident, loving parent to feel impatient, unsure, and at times even mean.

But we keep at it because discipline is also one of the most important parts of child rearing. Or so I try to remind myself when my one-year-old is unspooling the toilet paper, my three-year-old is saying "Poopy head!" because I turned off the VCR, and the six- and eight-year-olds are feuding again—all at the same time. My job as a parent isn't to keep them endlessly happy. (Much of what makes them happy, after all, involves making messes, breaking rules, and being unsociable.) Rather, my goal is to equip them to become pleasant, responsible individuals who know right from wrong and can exercise self-control.

All of that is easier said than done, of course. You've got to think quickly and act coolly in the heat of the moment. There are a million different situations that can come up, and it's impossible to handle every one of them flawlessly. What's helpful, however, is having a good understanding of the real purposes of discipline (no, it doesn't mean spanking) and a repertoire of effective, practical strategies to choose from. This book summarizes both. As a parent, I feel there's nothing like the input of experienced experts—other parents and professionals alike—to bolster my instincts and arm me with useful tactics to try. Hopefully, these ideas will do the same for you. The goal: parents who feel better about discipline and, ultimately, children who are better behaved.

—Paula Spencer

PARENTING

Guide to
Positive Discipline

CHAPTER ONE

Why
All Kids
Need It

What happens when you think about the word discipline? Do you feel your muscles tighten at the memory of last night's power struggle with your preschooler? Let loose an involuntary, exhausted sigh? Worry that you're too soft or too tough? Do you aim to be just like your own parents—or exactly the opposite? Do you feel pretty good about the way you handle the day-to-day challenges, but wonder, in the back of your mind, how everything's going to turn out in ten or twenty years?

Whatever your mind-set, you've probably given the subject of discipline plenty of thought. That's because it takes up a good deal of most parents' time.

Whether your child is a baby, a toddler, a preschooler or a kindergartener, how you discipline helps shape his or her life.

Laying the Groundwork Now

Discipline is a loaded subject for most parents. Few of us would pick it as the most enjoyable aspect of parenthood. In fact, it's usually more of a chore than a pleasure. Yet few aspects of child rearing are as important in determining what sort of person your child will grow up to be.

Unfortunately the very notion of child discipline suffers from an identity crisis. It's not as onerous a responsibility as it may sound. Ask a dozen parents how they do it, and you'll hear a dozen variations, with answers like, "We use time-outs." "I guess I yell a lot." Or, "We take away privileges." It's true that when we do those things we are disciplining a child. But they are merely disciplinary *tactics*. Discipline has come to be a sort of shorthand for punishment. And punishment is only one dimension of the big picture called discipline.

Punishment is a way to control your child. Discipline is a way to teach your child *self*-control.

Developing your child's self-discipline is the ultimate goal. It's a skill that your child can use her entire life. Self-control will make your child a more pleasant person to be around. Self-discipline is also what will get your child through the tumultuous teenage years, where she may step over the line at times, but be held in check by what she's learned early on.

The specific ways you discipline your child will vary as he grows. The advice in this book is tailored for *infancy through children six years of age*. These are the years when you lay the foundation for healthy discipline.

Ideally, discipline hinges more on cooperation than control. It's the values you instill, the social manners you convey, the way you treat your child, and how you teach him to treat other people and the world around him. Discipline is the way you teach him to *be* in the world.

In other words, discipline is not something done apart from the rest of child rearing. It *is* child rearing.

Punishment, on the other hand, requires a negative trigger—the child behaves badly, therefore you respond with punishment. Discipline requires positive triggers—you want your child to behave

DEFINITION

Discipline

Instruction; a subject that is taught; an orderly or prescribed conduct of behavior. To discipline a child is to teach him how to be well behaved; show him right from wrong; build his self-confidence and his respect for others; and teach him the self-control and *self-discipline* that can help him grow into the sort of person you want him to be.

4

well, therefore everything you do feeds that goal. Consider the two boxed definitions.

DEFINITION

Punishment

A penalty imposed on an offender for a fault, offense, or violation. To punish a child is to react to his poor behavior in a punitive way.

Children aren't born knowing the right way to behave. They need to learn everything—right from wrong, how to get along with others, which behaviors will get them what they want. They are as much in need of social and emotional guidance as they are in need of someone to fill their stomachs and wipe their bottoms. Your job is to show your child which behaviors are appropriate and which are not, and how to choose the right ones for himself.

Learning all this takes time—lots of time. Discipline isn't something that a parent can focus on a few hours a day or week, like taking a child to piano lessons. Nor is it a ten-step program to be mastered in a few easy lessons. Unfortunately, you can't even do it well in the early years and then let it slide once your child has the basics down pat. (Although, if you're persistent in the first five or six years, you're apt to be rewarded with smoother progress later.) Modifying anyone's behavior is a gradual process born of trial and error. Sometimes it's two steps forward, one step back.

Discipline requires endless practice, endless perseverance, and endless patience. As long as your child is under your wing, you'll be disciplining him or her.

The Goals of Healthy Discipline

What sort of child does every parent want? A good child, of course! *Good* is a subjective term, though. To some families, a good child is one who cleans his plate and goes to bed without kicking up a fuss. Elsewhere, a good child is one who simply manages to get through adolescence without a visit to juvenile court. The word *good* also implies an unsavory flip side: If there are good children, then there must also be bad children.

Yet lots of the behavior we think of as "bad" are perfectly normal. Tired toddlers tend to be cranky and negative. A four-year-old with a growing vocabulary and a vivid imagination spins amazing tall tales that, while technically are lies, are not intentionally hurtful. It's only when misbehavior goes unchecked that it tends to spiral out of control and become part of a child's personality, creating a bad situation.

CHECKLIST
Rethinking Discipline

Discipline Isn't . . .	Discipline Is . . .
✔ something you do *to* your child	✔ something that you do *with* your child
✔ a response to a problem	✔ a way of life
✔ just one thing	✔ many things
✔ about controlling	✔ about teaching *self*-control
✔ just for older kids	✔ something that begins in infancy
✔ an option	✔ an essential aspect of child rearing

Semantics aside, we all know a well-behaved child when we see one. Not a perfect child, who never makes a fuss or a mess—perfect children don't exist in the *real* world. A well-behaved child is one whose across-the-board behavior is generally good.

What does well-behaved mean to you? Ask yourself what personal qualities are important to you. What sort of person do you want your child to be when she is ten? Eighteen? Thirty-five? The list of potential adjectives you might string together is endless. Some traits (such as temperament) are inherited. But many others are shaped by the child's world. The way you discipline your child is one of the most potent behavior-shapers you have.

It starts with accentuating the positives, the goals that you are working toward.

The aim of healthy discipline should be to guide a child to become:

- **Respectful.** A child who understands the Golden Rule: Treat others as you would like to be treated yourself.

- **Responsible.** A child who can be trusted to do the right thing—which of course implies that he also knows the difference between right and wrong.

- **Unspoiled.** A child who is nurtured, loved, and given what he needs to grow—without being overindulged.

- **Obedient.** A child who understands the rules and knows how to abide by them.

- **Well-mannered.** A child who practices the social niceties, from saying "please" to helping someone in trouble.

- **Self-assured.** A child who feels secure and self-confident, with a healthy sense of herself and her self-worth.

- **Considerate.** A child who is sensitive to the feelings and concerns of others.

- **Honest.** A child who tells the truth.

- **Happy.** A child who enjoys life and is eager to explore, learn, and grow.

- **Pleasant to be around.** A child whom you not only love, but also *like*.

Feel free to embellish upon this list, which is by no means exhaustive. It's worth adding other qualities that you value and wish to impart.

Why Kids Misbehave

No matter how diligent you are, sooner or later the little apple of your eye will defy you. And it will happen sooner rather than later. She will sass back, squeeze all of the toothpaste out of the tube, scream at the top of her lungs in the middle of the grocery store, hit her baby brother. *All* children misbehave. A child who behaves perfectly all the time and has done so for his entire life exists only in the imagination (or on Nick at Nite reruns!). Kids *need* to test you—it's in their very makeup to act up occasionally.

Why is a certain amount of misbehavior to be expected? Here are some of the reasons that kids act up:

- **Kids misbehave in order to learn.** To help them understand what behavior is acceptable, children need to define what's *un*acceptable. It's not enough for them to hear the rules as issued by their parents. They also have to test those rules for themselves and push the limits in order to determine what really is okay and what isn't. It's also you who's being tested: *If I do this, what will Mom or Dad do?*

- **Kids misbehave to get attention.** Above all, a child wants her parents' affection and approval. The desire to please is a deep motivator. A child will do what the parent wants (that is, behave well) in order to gain attention. But negative attention is as valuable to a child as positive attention. If he doesn't sense your focus and approval when he's acting nicely, he'll settle for the shouting or fuss he can conjure up by being naughty. At least when a child is being punished, he's certain that he has his parents' undivided concentration. Sibling rivalry is another form of competitive misbehavior in the quest for parents' love—to get more love than the other sibling receives, as if that could be measured.

- **Kids misbehave to exert their individuality.** This is especially true of toddlers and young preschoolers, who have begun to realize that they are people in their own right, distinct from Mom and Dad. They say "yes" when you say "no" or "stop" when you say "go." And they do so *just because.* They are exploring their powers and sorting out what they are capable of.

- **Kids misbehave because they want reassurance that you're in charge.** Despite their occasional bravado and ever-increasing size, kids are kids. You are big and they are small. Just as your child looks to you for sustenance and love, he depends on you to keep him safe in the world. Talking back and seeing that you won't come unglued is strangely comforting. It reassures your child that all is right in the natural order of things. Of course, he's not sophisticated enough to see it exactly this way, but that's what he's feeling in his bones.

- **Kids misbehave because their development and their parents' expectations are out of sync.** A two-year-old is not physically capable of sitting quietly through a five-course meal. So he fidgets, whines, or begins tossing forks or knocking over water glasses. It's misbehavior by an adult's standards (or by standards appropriate for an eight-year-old), but for a toddler such actions are merely a way to channel natural energy and curiosity. No, sending forks flying isn't acceptable. But by the same token, sitting still for two hours is not developmentally within a toddler's repertoire.

- **Kids misbehave when they can't think how else to act.** Sometimes a child is simply not yet equipped with the social or language skills to more gracefully navigate a situation. A toddler may have a tantrum because she can't quickly string together the words to convey her feelings. A preschooler who feels his space being invaded by a bigger, stronger child lashes out to defend himself in the first way that comes to mind—with his teeth. Such instances aren't willful disobedience; they're reactions to a specific situation.

- **Kids misbehave when they are tired, sick, or hungry.** It's no coincidence that whining revs up when naptime is overdue. Or that a child loses it in the grocery store, surrounded by so many delicious temptations, as his lunch hour approaches. It's difficult for anyone to have his act together completely when he's not functioning at 100 percent. Why should your child be any different?

- **Kids misbehave because they haven't been taught any better.** It's only natural: Children persist in using behavior that goes uncorrected. They're also more apt to continue undesirable behavior if they are sometimes corrected but sometimes ignored. It's like playing the lottery: If whining worked yesterday, though not the day before, why not try it again just in case it will get me what I want today?

These explanations don't excuse bad behavior. But they provide useful perspective. Understanding the "why" goes a long way toward reducing your frustration and developing your patience—important tools to help you guide your child in a better direction.

The Eight Essential Elements

Once the basic components of healthy discipline are in place, life is easier for everyone. For the child, they provide the secure base from which good behavior can grow. And for the parent, that means fewer hassles and headaches.

The eight essential elements to achieving healthy discipline are:

1. *Outlook:* Having the right attitude toward discipline. Think of guiding your child's behavior as giving him a gift—the gift of self-control and, eventually, self-sufficiency.

2. *Expectations:* Having a realistic sense of your child's personality and abilities. It also means making your expectations clear to your child.

3. *Limits:* Setting limits so your child understands the boundaries of acceptable behavior—and the consequences of stepping beyond those boundaries.

4. *Consistency:* Enforcing those limits and their consequences firmly and consistently.

5. *Routines:* Giving your child a secure base for learning and growing by establishing a predictable household rhythm.

6. *Anticipation:* Setting up your child's behavior for success.

7. *Examples:* Demonstrating desirable behavior in your own everyday life.

8. *Love and Respect:* Treating your child the way you would want to be treated and giving him unconditional love and support—no matter what he does, you will always love him for who he *is*.

How do these elements work in everyday life?

1. Outlook

Discipline starts in your head. The idea of spending eighteen years relentlessly training your child to be an obedient, model citizen can feel burdensome. So don't look at it that way. Instead, look at discipline as the way you plan to instill good values in your child. Your ultimate goal should be for him to develop self-discipline, the ability to conduct himself in the "right" way all by himself. Think of yourself as a tour guide, not a drill sergeant.

Imagine your child as an alien that has been dropped from space, or as a visitor from a foreign land. She doesn't know the language or customs, and is dependent upon you to show her the way. What is the correct behavior here? How should your visitor behave in the zillions of new circumstances in which she'll find herself? How do people here treat one another? What's considered helpful, kind, and good? What should she value? She turns to you for counsel and care, so you want to take care to teach her these things without being intimidating or frightening. You don't want to squelch her natural enthusiasm for this new world or undermine the way she thinks about herself. At the same time, you don't want to do anything to make her mistrust you or chafe against your guidance. She'll learn by trial and error, and by relying on your reactions to her behavior. But if she is to thrive in her new world, it will be because you've collaborated as leader and follower—which is different from being ruler and subject.

Don't expect to do your part flawlessly. As a tour guide, you can't expect to know all the answers, no matter how quick you are to react to pinched siblings and back talk. Guiding a child's behavior is a relentless, and often thankless, task. The upside is that going into child rearing knowing that your goal is a "good" child, not a perfect one, will make it easier for you and your child. Kids are never perfect. But then, neither are parents—so why expect more of your child than you do of yourself?

What about all those friends' and neighbors' kids who seem to behave perfectly? Rest assured that you're not seeing the full picture of their lives. Resist comparisons to ideals (which are almost always imaginary). Use only your own standards as your yardstick. Guiding your child to maturity requires eighteen years of patience, and plenty of persistence. Kids don't automatically learn something new on the first try. Often they'll make the same mistakes again and again before a lesson is absorbed.

Of course, *good* is a loaded word, too. Children may be born innocent, but they are not innately good. Goodness is a learned skill, a tedious process of figuring out how to conduct oneself in a dizzying variety of circumstances. A toddler has no natural understanding of the difference between a tone of voice to be used indoors and a louder voice that is more appropriate for outdoors. A three-year-old wasn't born knowing that he shouldn't lick the frosting off the cake on the counter, or that the wonderful toys in the store must be paid for before they can be pocketed and taken home. These things must be learned. It's important to keep reminding yourself that misbehavior is normal. Perfectly, utterly, absolutely normal. A child who rarely makes a misstep tends to be one who is painfully shy, fearful, or stressed out as a result of pressures to "be good." A child who sometimes shouts, hits, knocks things over, or writes on places crayons were not meant to be used is normal. This doesn't mean that such behaviors should go unacknowledged. It simply means that your child is typical—and ripe for learning a better way.

Recognize that mischief and misdeeds are merely the flip sides of curiosity and adorableness.

Discipline becomes far less intimidating when you can think of it not as something done separately from the rest of child rearing, but as simply more threads of the whole tapestry.

Remember:

- No parent is perfect.
- No child is perfect.
- You're a guide, not a cop.
- Discipline takes time.

2. Expectations

Much of parents' frustration can be averted by having realistic expectations of their child. This means taking into account her age and developmental stage, along with the circumstances. Raise the bar too high and your child is bound to stumble. For example, a preschooler attempting to play a board game made for children five years of age and up may not understand the intricacies of the rules. As she grows increasingly impatient at being told how to play, she's liable to throw the board on the floor in frustration. Sometimes behavior that's age-appropriate is mislabeled as misbehavior.

You have the right to expect certain standards of behavior of your children. Even the littlest talkers can be taught to say "please" and "thank you" (although they may not use these words consistently and without prompting), but a five-year-old may not be ready to greet strangers with a formal handshake and a "How do you do?" Unless your standards are rooted in realism, you're bound to be disappointed, and perhaps may be unfairly harsh with your child as a result.

You can get a pretty good idea of your child's capabilities by being observant when you spend time with him. Or watch the way he and other children his age interact at birthday parties, the park, preschool, or day care. Reading books or magazine articles about child development can also help focus your picture of what's typical at given ages. Remember, too, that children develop at different rates. They don't all learn to talk or walk or kick a ball at exactly the same age. So leave some leeway for individuality and avoid the added pressure of comparisons between children.

Having realistic expectations of your child requires a certain amount of nimbleness. Kids change as they grow. You'll want to maintain a balance between continuing to challenge his increasing abilities without overwhelming him by making things too difficult. For example, a three-year-old may lack the coordination to completely set the table, but she can put out napkins and forks, and you can add on responsibilities as she gets older.

In addition to being realistic about a child's capabilities, parents also need to have clear expectations about their behavior. These should be based on the child's age and developmental stage. For example, by the time your child is walking, he's ready for household and safety rules: No touching the stove because it might be hot. Always hold a grown-up's hand when crossing the street. As your child grows, these should increase in number and complexity: Dirty dishes should be brought to the sink when you're finished eating. Put away one toy before you take out another one. If you haven't defined which rules you're adamant about, you'll have trouble enforcing them consistently.

It's equally important to communicate your expectations to your child. This can be done through your actions as well as your words. You steer your toddler away from the electrical outlets and gently tell her, "Not for baby." You escort your preschooler back into the bathroom and ask him to turn off the faucet that he left running. You take away a plate of food that's being toyed with by a kindergartener and ask, "Are you finished and ready to be excused now?"

Remember:

- Be sure your expectations for your child are developmentally realistic.
- Expectations should evolve as your child grows.
- Be consistent about what you expect.
- Communicate your expectations to your child.

3. Limits

Limit is a restrictive-sounding word. The word means something that bounds, restrains, or confines. It conjures up images of rigid law enforcers rather than benevolent tour guides. But even tour guides must keep their charges away from hostile, dangerous places and borders for which they have no passports.

CHECKLIST
What Can You Expect at Different Ages?

The following examples provide merely thumbnail sketches, but they illustrate how a parent's expectations need to evolve along with her child.

Infants: Birth to One

✔ Newborns cry to communicate all their needs.

✔ Infants need to be held often to develop a sense of security.

✔ Infants explore through their senses, including mouthing and tasting.

✔ Infants cannot understand rules; it's up to you to anticipate their needs or respond to them, and to make their world safe.

✔ By four to six months of age, they can learn to wait brief intervals to be fed or changed. They can begin to sleep through the night without a feeding.

✔ By one year, they no longer require immediate gratification and can begin to learn to wait for food. They can begin to feed themselves at mealtime.

Toddlers: One to Three Years Old

✔ Are active explorers and require a safe environment in which to learn.

✔ Need consistent routines to provide a sense of calm.

✔ Are discovering their own self-power and prefer to make their own simple choices.

✔ Are prone to tantrums because they lack both verbal skills to express themselves and physical skills to accomplish all they want to do.

✔ Can begin to dress themselves and handle simple self-care.

✔ Can start to learn simple rules.

✔ Aren't ready to understand sharing.

✔ Are usually ready to begin learning to use the toilet around age two-and-a-half, though success may not follow for another year or more.

Preschoolers: Three to Five Years Old

✔ Have boundless curiosity and appetite for learning; they need an environment that is safe, stimulating, and challenging.

✔ Thrive on routine and predictability.

✔ Still have tantrums as they struggle between wanting the comforts of a smaller child and having the freedoms of a bigger one.

✔ Are rapidly developing newfound abilities; can dress themselves, wash themselves, brush their teeth, prepare simple snacks.

✔ Are capable of distinguishing right from wrong.

✔ Can begin to understand logic and consequences.

✔ Can follow rules.

✔ Are notoriously egocentric, but are developing a sense of empathy for others.

✔ Are good at cooperative learning, sharing, and working with others.

✔ Can learn how to solve their own disagreements.

✔ Can be reasoned with.

✔ Continue to test limits as they gain new skills and freedoms.

✔ Are ready for household responsibilities, if they haven't begun them earlier.

✔ Begin turning to peers and other influences outside the family for ideas and role models, and may test or rebel against family influences as a result.

Older children: Six Years Old and Up

✔ Are struggling to develop a sense of competence; require support and encouragement as much as younger children.

Restrictions are a good thing. For one thing, they keep a child safe: *No running with scissors. No swimming without an adult present.* Limits keep others safe: *Hitting hurts. If you throw sand, you have to leave the sandbox.*

Limits also serve a vital role in civilizing a child. It's hard, if not impossible, for a child to know what he's supposed to do unless he also has a sense of what he's *not* supposed to do. Setting limits for your child does as much to define good behavior as it does to cordon off the bad.

Don't worry that you'll curb your child's free spirit. Her wonderful innate curiosity isn't going to shrivel up and vanish. In fact, setting limits feeds your child's sense of security. Kids like rules—even if they don't always act as if they do. Your child may fuss at being told it's time for his bath or complain about the TV being turned off, but the absence of such guidelines tends to create uneasiness. A child is never sure where he stands. It's a little like creeping over a minefield, unsure when you'll make a fatal mistake because you have no map to guide you safely across the terrain. It's frightening.

Limits typically take the form of rules: No biting. No TV before school. No blowing bubbles into your milk. Whatever rules you decide on, make them as clear and specific as possible. You'll probably need to repeat them over and over, until your child begins to internalize them. Try to phrase them positively, if possible: "Ask first before opening the refrigerator." "Let your guest have a turn first." "If you get urine on the toilet seat, you have to clean it up." "Crayons are for paper only, not for tables."

Giving your child clear limits also communicates volumes about your values. They let a child know what you think about such concepts as responsibility, sharing, and tolerance. They also let your child know what your family considers important—attending church? Community service? Education? Sports?

To be effective, rules need to be reasonable. Knee-jerk declarations that make little sense—"Get your shoes on right this minute or we're not going to the party"—are seldom respected. Neither are those issued arbitrarily, with little thought to the situation at hand ("No running in the park!"). One way to get children to respect rules is to involve them in the process. Explain the "why" behind a rule, using the simplest language for younger children. "We don't run in the house in stocking feet because we might slip and fall and get hurt." "You can't eat cookies right now because it's almost time for dinner. The cookies will fill your stomach and you won't be hungry for dinner food, which helps you grow and be strong."

CHECKLIST
Some Rules About Rules

✔ Make them age-appropriate and realistic.

✔ Let your child know the rules ahead of time through reminders and warnings.

✔ Enforce them consistently.

✔ Don't hesitate or waver when enforcing rules, even when you're sick or tired.

✔ Specific is better than vague. ("Don't shout," rather than "Be sweet.")

✔ Explain the reason for the rule. ("Biting hurts.")

✔ Attach reasonable consequences. ("If you turn on the TV without asking, you won't be allowed to watch it at all today.")

✔ Enlist your child's involvement. ("Tell me what happens when we run at the pool?")

✔ Follow family rules yourself.

✔ Expect rules to be tested, defied, forgotten, and broken. It's normal.

✔ Be prepared to repeat rules often. Learning them is a gradual process.

Tailor your message to your child. Young children benefit from very specific results if you break the process into manageable tasks: "Put all your clothes in the hamper. Then put your toys in the toy box." A child who has difficulty making transitions between activities would benefit from warm-up suggestions: "After you put your shoes on we will go to the park."

Limits are great—within limits. A child who hears an endless litany of rules all through the day is apt to tune them out. Resist the temptation to jump in with endless warnings and reminders. Let your child make her own choices and figure some things out for herself, if she's in no danger of harm. This helps develop a budding sense of responsibility. Creating a safe environment for play through childproofing is important because you eliminate the need to hover and say no. Realize, too, that not all limits need to be expressed as rules. While every family has its own specific guidelines, such as "No eating in the living room," you also have many standards of behavior that defy simple descriptions, such as "Be nice to others." Your child learns to live up to these standards through your example, rather than by your constant reminders. Rules should evolve as your child grows.

Remember:

- All kids need rules.
- Limits help keep kids safe and feeling secure.
- Limits are also a way to telegraph your values and to define desirable behavior.
- Limits should be both spoken and unspoken.

4. Consistency

Setting limits is only half the story. It is equally necessary to enforce them. Alas, this is the tougher part of the deal. Effectively enforcing limits requires firmness and consistency. Too often parents are reluctant to deny their child or are in a rush and lack the time or energy to enforce limits in a consistent way. This in turn only makes things more difficult.

How would you feel if the traffic laws or income tax changed from day to day and without notice? On the one hand you might be tempted to see what you could get away with—if the shortcuts you took yesterday will work again today. On the other hand, you'd also feel a certain amount of added uncertainty and stress as a result.

A rule loses its punch if it is applied only sporadically. Your child thinks, *If I was able to do that yesterday, why can't I do it again today?* You can bet she'll try. Likewise, she'll be confused if you punish her for the very same activity that she watched you condone only the day before. It's hardest to be consistent when you're tired or stressed out. Unfortunately, these are some of the times when kids act up most. Example: The "witching hour" before dinner, when parents and children are being reunited after a day at work and day care or school. Everyone's a bit tired and hungry, and the children are understandably excited to see their parents. They want your attention. But the dinner preparations, the mail, the dog, and lingering thoughts about a crisis at work are also crowding your mind. Seeing that he has competition for your attention, your child will most likely choose this time to squabble, break rules, or otherwise exasperate you. It's tempting to ignore bad behavior at moments like these. Yet this is precisely when you need to have your child toe the line.

For similar reasons, it's best to respond immediately. Don't put it off until *you* feel more settled or until there's a more convenient time.

You should also be relatively consistent in how you treat more than one child in a family. Although you want to make allowances for their different ages, general house rules should be observed by everyone. Allowing one child to get away with something that another is reprimanded for will be perceived as playing favorites.

Spell out the consequences of defying limits just as clearly as you've set up the rules. Consequences help a child decide whether breaking a rule is worth the risk. One of the best motivators is your attention—the prize kids value above all. That's why a time-out (see page 88) is often an effective tool. Ditto taking away privileges, even if it's only removing a special toy from play for a set period of time.

Consequences should also be consistent. Use time-outs for the same few reasons—for example, preferably for serious misdeeds, such as hitting—and not as a one-size-fits-all punishment. Ideally, the consequences should fit the crime. Minor transgressions should be dealt with less severely than more serious misdeeds. If your corrective action is related to the behavior, it can help to underscore your message. For example, if two five-year-olds are fighting over a toy truck, you can ask them to resolve the problem between themselves, perhaps suggesting that they take turns with the truck. But if the squabbling continues you can warn them that the truck will have to be removed altogether.

Being firm and consistent isn't the same as being rigid and inflexible. Trust your judgment. When your child is sick, for instance, you might relax house rules about when and how much TV may be watched. If it's been raining for two weeks straight, there's no harm in letting your child practice gymnastics in the middle of the living room floor.

Remember:

- Be firm.
- Act swiftly.
- Issue consequences consistently.
- Don't let slide today what was not allowed yesterday.
- However, consistency doesn't mean something written in stone— sometimes there's a good reason to make an exception.

5. Routines

Think of them as the invisible force. Routines are the daily rhythms that families come to take for granted. Mealtimes. Bedtimes. Who does what. What happens when. When families with young children have lots of routines, everyone benefits. Routines set up a framework for the day. They provide expectations everyone can follow, which is especially useful when kids can't tell time. They neutralize many potentially hot issues and eliminate the need to negotiate endlessly about certain everyday events.

Above all, routines arm children with a sense of security. A child who can count on the basics doesn't need to worry about when she'll get fed or what the day will bring. She knows that breakfast follows waking up and getting dressed; that Daddy will take her to school and Mommy will be there to pick her up; that storytime will come before bedtime, and so forth. These routines eliminate uncertainty, which puts her in a better frame of mind to focus on other things. The sense of predictability that routines engender also underscores a child's sense of faith, trust, and love in her parents. Because her parents meet her primary needs without comment or complaint, she knows they will be there for her, no matter what.

Another way to foster security is through little rituals. Perhaps your family has pizza night every Wednesday. Or you have a special way to signal "I love you" before departure at day care in the mornings. Or you call Grandma every Saturday. To a young child, a ritual can be as simple as wearing a certain sweater to the park or saying good night to stuffed animals in a particular order. Sometimes parents overlook the value of rituals, concentrating instead on providing bigger special moments for their kids. Yet when it comes to a child's sense of well-being, small routines pack even more punch than grand gestures like a trip to a theme park or an impromptu ice-cream cone.

Routines are not meant to be carved in stone, however. The idea isn't to be a slave to them. Instead, aim to let routines work for you, as a tool to make your day run more smoothly and efficiently. If a special occasion dictates that naptime be missed, the bottom isn't going to drop out of your child's world. If dinner is late or Mom has to go out of town on a business trip, your child will survive just fine. The important thing about rituals is that they become the norm. The occasional exception won't undo everything.

Remember:

- Kids need routines.

- Kids *want* routines.
- Routines make discipline easier.
- Routines should be dependable but bendable.

6. Anticipation

It's important to figure out where your child tends to have problems and set up signposts and escape routes to help him stay on the right path. There are many ways you can set your child up for success by sidestepping potential disciplinary snags. One way is to respect those predictable routines. Don't drag a small child on a string of ten different errands on a Saturday and expect bliss. Instead, pare your list to two or three errands. Arm yourself with

CHECKLIST
Smart Routines Every Household Needs

Even if you're the go-with-the-flow type, it's hard to argue with the many benefits a predictable schedule provides a young child. Routines to consider include:

✔ **Regular mealtimes.** Eat at approximately the same time every day, including snacks.

✔ **Regular sleeping times.** Your child should get up at about the same time every day, and have a consistent bedtime. Naps should also fall at regular times. A child who must be roused awake every morning is probably not going to bed early enough.

✔ **A regular sleeping place.** Better not to let kids nap in the car or wherever they happen to collapse.

✔ **Mealtime connections.** Try to eat at least one meal a day together as a family. But don't make a young child sit still at the table longer than is realistic. Avoid on-the-go meals eaten in the car.

✔ **Bedtime routines.** Aim for ten to twenty minutes of predictable events, such as toothbrushing followed by two books followed by a kiss and tucking in. Keep the sequence of events manageable. If you have to write it all down for a babysitter or it takes more than half an hour, you're trying too hard.

✔ **Weekend routines.** Sometimes it's hard to match the weekdays hour for hour, but try to maintain consistency regarding meals, naps, and bedtime.

diversions such as a small toy for the child to play with. Take a break in the park for twenty minutes before tackling any more tasks.

Advance planning can also prepare your child for unfamiliar experiences. Before visiting a relative who lives far away, for example, provide some gentle coaching that goes beyond a blanket "Be good." You might say, "When we get there, I'd like for you to give your aunt a hello—you could hug her or shake her hand. Then we'll sit and talk for a while, so you'll need to use a quieter 'inside' voice; no yelling. I won't be able to play with you or watch everything you do. You'll need to sit and play with the doll and puzzles that you brought, and then we will have a snack." By running through a script of the upcoming event, your child is better prepared to know how to act. You can do the same thing before heading into a store loaded with temptations. Say, "We are going to buy groceries, not candy. I will let you help me put things in the cart and choose which kind of cereal you want. But if you make a fuss about candy, we will have to leave." Make sure your child understands the plan—and be prepared to follow through if she does act up.

Involving your child in decision-making can also circumvent potential problems. If he balks over getting dressed, give a choice: "Do you want to wear this red shirt or this blue one?" Find ways to compromise. Out of habit, parents often find themselves standing firm on issues where the outcome really makes no big difference. Does your two-year-old really need to wear shoes in the house? Is it absolutely necessary that your four-year-old cleans his plate before he eats dessert? Make the choices manageable, so that they don't overwhelm. And take care not to turn every situation into fodder for your child's input. Too many decisions can be stressful. You are the adult here. Limit choices to innocuous matters that make little difference to you but that seem to have a lot of importance to your child. By enlisting your child's own decision-making powers where feasible, you can avoid letting issues spiral into a power struggle.

Anticipating problems doesn't mean making life as easy as possible for your child. The idea isn't to do everything for your child in order to smooth the way. Kids *need* challenges. They also need to experience disappointment and failure. If your six-year-old forgets her lunch every day, but you then drive to the school and deliver it, she has no incentive to try harder to remember it tomorrow. She's not going to go hungry, because she knows you'll bail her out. Instead, you might work with your child to figure out ways she can better remember her lunch: By putting it next to the door where it can't be missed? By writing herself a reminder note?

Likewise, advance planning beats giving in when a toddler pitches a fit in a drugstore because you won't buy him a candy cane. As his cries grow more shrill and passers-by begin to look your way, you become more embarrassed. But you're waiting for your prescription to be filled and don't want to beat a hasty retreat now. You plead with your son to calm down, but his shrieks just turn louder. Now he's hurled himself onto the floor and people are really staring. So, you say, "Okay! Here's the candy cane you wanted! Now shush!" Your son is no longer disappointed, but he has learned nothing from the situation other than that Mom can be manipulated and screaming is an effective way to get what he wants. You can be sure he'll try it again. Better to have distracted him with some graham crackers stashed in your purse, or to have called ahead to make sure the prescription would be ready by the time you arrived.

Having patience also helps improve the odds of success. Toddlers do some things—zipping a coat, following you out the door—excruciatingly slowly. Preschoolers spill juice and can't seem to help making messes. Resist the temptation to snap or to complete the task at hand yourself. Instead, arm your child for success. Anchor the bottom of the zipper for your child while she pulls it up, or attach a large, easy-to-grasp zipper pull to her coat. Hold your tongue when your preschooler makes a spill. Instead, show her how to mop it up, so when it happens again you can just hand her a towel and clean up together. Patience also comes in handy when you're issuing the hundredth reminder and feel ready to explode. Kids often need to do something over and over again before they learn it. With your persistence, however, they one day will.

Remember:

- An ounce of prevention is worth a ton of headaches.
- Coach your child in what's expected of him.
- Offer reasonable choices.
- Don't attempt to smooth every rough patch in your child's life.
- Patience really is a virtue.

7. Examples

Actions really do speak louder than words when it comes to children. There's nothing like becoming a parent to make you watch your step. You

My child sees me do something that's wrong, like swear?

Own up to your mistake. Say something like, "I shouldn't have said that. It wasn't a polite word. I was angry. Using that word didn't accomplish anything and didn't make me feel better." If you say nothing, your child is bound to remember the incident and add the word to his vocabulary, without having an appropriate context for it. A common impulse after a curse word slips out is to hastily add, "Don't let me ever hear *you* use that word!" This, however, only makes the word alluring to your child. It also shuts down further conversation about the subject. It sends the message that it's all right for you to use bad words but your child cannot, while the real message you want to impart is that no one should use such language because it's unkind.

can be sure that she's observing everything you say and do and filing away those collected images for later retrieval.

We've all seen parents contradict themselves while attempting to correct a child. There's the father who spanks his son and admonishes, "No hitting, do you understand?" The mother who yells back at her screaming child in the grocery store. Such blunders would be comical, if they weren't so counterproductive.

Some examples are less direct, but also less than helpful. It's confusing, for example, for a child to overhear her parent telling a neighbor a little white lie—"I'm sorry I can't come over right now; Jane is about to take a nap." Making snappish comments at bad drivers may help you let off steam, but does nothing to help your child understand how to treat his fellow man.

Also avoid putting yourself above family rules. If kids aren't allowed to snarf ice cream in the living room, then the grown-ups shouldn't either. If curse words are verboten, don't curse. If attending church is important, the entire family should go. Let your child see you treating other people with courtesy and kindness. Don't argue with your mate when the kids can see (or hear). Don't grab. Don't yell. Don't have a tantrum yourself.

Remember:

- You're being watched.
- Your actions often carry more clout than your words.
- Being a good role model is not just a cliche, it's a responsibility.

8. Love and Respect

Perhaps the greatest gift that a parent can give a child is unconditional love. Unconditional means *no strings attached*. You cherish your child for who he is, not for who you want him to be or hope he will be or wish that he was, if only he would try harder. You might not like everything he does—the messy room, the broken vase, the threats he makes to his little sister—but you still love him. This requires keeping your critical focus on the actions, not the person.

Part of loving your child is respecting him. Mutual respect comes before obedience. It means treating your child at all times like the human being that he is. It means treating him the way you like to be treated yourself. Only when you're attuned to his interests, needs, and concerns can you effectively discipline him, because only then will he appreciate that you have his best interests at heart. Acknowledge his feelings: "You must feel angry because your sister is sick and we can't go to the playground. I know that's a big disappointment for you. Would you like me to get out the special paints instead and we can paint together while she naps?"

It's hard to show respect for someone and yell at them at the same time. Ditto for threatening, belittling, and ridiculing.

Loving your child doesn't mean making everything smooth and perfect. The idea behind healthy discipline is that you love your child enough to see that establishing limits and enforcing them consistently will truly benefit him. It means you love him enough to do all you can to set him up for success, but realize that success or failure is sometimes a choice that your child must make on his own.

Remember:

- Love your child for who he is.
- Treat your child the way you would like to be treated yourself.
- Love your child enough to be firm.
- Love your child enough to let him suffer consequences in order to learn from them.

Is My Child Spoiled?

Spoiling is the point at which nurturing slides into overindulging. Rather than merely giving a child what he needs, we give him more than he needs—*lots* more. How will you know when your child is spoiled? You will. Spoiled kids tend to be fussy, demanding, defiant, and tyrannical. They're not happy—but it's not their fault. Children who are spoiled have been trained to behave that way.

Most parents begin to worry about spoiling during infancy. For example, they've heard that they shouldn't hold their baby too much. Being new at

HOT TOPIC

Developing Responsibility

An important part of healthy discipline is instilling a sense of responsibility in your child. Setting and enforcing firm limits helps a child understand what your expectations are. In turn, she's more likely to live up to those expectations. It's no surprise that responsible children tend to grow up to be responsible adults.

Where well-intentioned parents sometimes veer off course is in underestimating their child's capabilities. It's easy to view a young child as a helpless creature who needs to have many things done for her. Obviously, she does—at first. But children grow and learn at an astounding rate, and it's a parent's job to keep up with those advances. You're doing your child no favors by, say, continuing to spoon-feed him at age 2 or clearing his plate from the table at age 4, when the child is able to do those things for himself.

Start setting realistic challenges for your child early in life. Give a nine-month-old a spoon at meals. Encourage a one-year-old who has begun to talk to say "please" and "thank you." Let your two-year-old retrieve a fresh diaper and throw the wet one away, and your child will come to think of such tasks as part of everyday life. When introducing a new task, show how it's done and then step back and let your child try for himself. It helps if you model responsible behavior—saying "please" yourself, for example, and doing chores such as vacuuming or setting the table with a cheerful demeanor.

Should you pay your child an allowance for carrying out responsibilities? It's your call. Certainly payment should not be set up for every job that your child has. Having responsibilities is part of life. You want to communicate the idea that many things must be done in a household simply because they need to be done. They're part of being a family member, of being an accountable person. If you convey the fact that virtues are their own reward, then there's no reason to reward a child monetarily for bringing in his bicycle into the garage before a rainstorm, for example.

Some experts recommend introducing an allowance around age 5 or 6. Few children understand the value of money or are motivated by it before then. Whether you tie the allowance to additional chores above and beyond your child's routine responsibilities is up to you. Many kids don't receive an allowance until they are older, and then only as an exercise in money management. A child can grow up fine without ever having one, too.

Some families find it useful to create a job chart, whether or not allowance is paid. Household responsibilities are clearly blocked out on a calendar that describes which tasks are done daily (such as making one's bed) and which are done periodically. A chart can be a useful, neutral reminder that takes the place of parental harping. Its usefulness is limited to a child who can read, though.

parenthood, it's hard to know how much of anything is "too much." Rest assured, however, that before ages 3 to 4 months, it's impossible to spoil a child. In fact, newborns benefit from being held often and having their cries responded to promptly.

Around 3 to 4 months, a baby learns that his cries will get attention. You should check on your child when he fusses, but not necessarily rush to pick him up at every whimper. Certainly if he is very uncomfortable, he should be comforted. But beginning at this age, babies often fall into the habit of wanting to be carried everywhere. They fuss when they are put down. This is an especially common behavior pattern for firstborn children, who have their parents' undivided attention. Babies do need stimulation, but they also benefit from occasional solitude. Get in the habit of putting your baby down throughout the day on a blanket on the floor with a few toys, in her crib with a busy box or mobile, or in a bouncy seat where she can watch you.

Between the ages of six and fifteen months, sleep problems often begin as a result of overindulgence. Babies begin to fuss when they are put to bed because of separation anxiety, teething, or because night feedings have become a habit (as opposed to a physical need). Parents hurry back to console.

CHECKLIST
Chores for Beginners

Here are some ways your child could begin to assume household responsibilities:

✓ **Age 2:** Wash hands, brush teeth (with assistance), clean up spills, help cook (pouring flour into mix, stirring sauces)

✓ **Age 3:** Dress self, put dirty clothes in hamper, hang up own coat, pick up toys, put napkins on table

✓ **Age 4:** Fold laundry, help empty dishwasher, straighten bedcovers, water plants, carry light groceries from car, remove own plate from table after eating

✓ **Age 5:** Tidy room, sort laundry, use broom and dustpan, plant flowers, pour own beverage, help set table

✓ **Age 6:** Empty garbage pails on trash day, feed or groom a pet, prepare own snack or sandwich, take own bath (with minor supervision), read to younger children

WHAT IF...

You hate the idea of being a disciplinarian?

Like it or not, it's part of the job description that you signed up for when you brought your little bundle of joy home from the hospital. *Disciplinarian* is a tough word, conjuring up for many parents memories of a strict parent or teacher who made their lives miserable. Don't get hung up on semantics. Think of yourself as a parent who wants his or her child to grow up safe, happy, secure, kind, well-adjusted, socially adept, and self-assured. That's not so terrible, is it?

The child is rocked or fed back to sleep. Some parents even lie down with their child until she falls asleep. All's well—until the child wakes again in the middle of the night, as all humans normally do in their sleep cycles, or until the next night. Then the child cries again because she wants the company repeated. Parents can avoid such vicious cycles by not perpetuating the habit in the first place. Don't rush in the baby's room at the first whimper. If crying persists, often the child can be soothed with your voice, either talking to her or singing a lullaby, but not actually picking her up.

Opportunities to spoil increase as your child grows. For one thing, they're so adorable and affectionate that the impulse to indulge is great. You want to give them as much as you can. Indulgence is not the same as spoiling, though. You can give your child treats and special favors, while sticking to the basic principles of healthy discipline, which will prevent you from becoming overindulgent.

Sometimes the challenge feels more difficult for working parents or divorced parents, who can't spend as much time with their children as they'd like. Guilt tends to creep in: "Am I giving my child enough? Is she happy?" They may feel reluctant to do anything that would be upsetting to their child, or do anything that might be construed as rejection. "Why make our limited time together a drag?" goes the rationale. In lieu of time, some parents lavish gifts and treats. While such extravagances surely please a child, the luster is short-lived. Then the child wants to know what's next, or begins to press demands for other, greater gifts, as sort of a challenge to the parent, a test of her love. The child learns to confuse possessions with love.

Excessive gift-giving inspires materialism and greed but doesn't have any lasting effect on happiness. Your child would rather have your undivided attention when you get home than five minutes with you and three hours with a new toy.

Another side effect of guilt is to be lax about the child's chores and responsibilities. Or a parent may feel reluctant to enforce a lot of rules. But sparing your child disappointment and labor is simply another form of overindulgence.

Children are smart enough to respond to both love and limits. Here are more tips for raising an unspoiled child:

- Establish clear limits.
- Enforce them without wavering.
- Recognize the difference between what your child needs and what he wants.
- Don't give in to whining, begging, or tantrums.
- Shower your child with attention, not things.
- Remember that it's not your job to keep your child happy 100 percent of the time.
- Keep in mind that kids appreciate authority and limits (even if they don't always act like it).

CHAPTER TWO

What's Your Discipline Style?

You wear your hair a certain way. You favor a certain look in the clothes you wear. You probably lean to the left or the right when it comes to various social and political policies. So it only makes sense that you have—or you'll gradually develop—a unique discipline style as well.

Your discipline style will influence the way you handle various situations regarding your child. Complicating matters, no two people's disciplinary approaches are exactly the same. So the other adults in your child's world—his other parent, his grandparents, his babysitter, his preschool teacher—may not always see eye-to-eye with you.

Which Shoe Fits?

What's your style? Every parent is different. So is every child. And every situation. How's that for an infinite number of variables? Your outlook and reactions are shaped by your own upbringing, personality, and temperament as well as your feelings about parenthood and your lifestyle. Add to this the fact that your partner brings his or her own discipline style to the table. In the best of circumstances, these philosophies are in sync. In the worst, they're continually at odds. Most likely, your approaches to discipline fall somewhere in the middle. On some issues you see eye-to-eye; others set the stage for disagreements. Finally, your child's temperament will influence how you handle him.

There is no single right way to discipline. A stubborn child responds to certain techniques differently than a compliant child. A cup of spilled milk doesn't warrant the same kind of intervention as hitting one's baby sister with a bat. You'll need to develop a number of strategies to handle different scenarios.

Because of the vast number of variables at play, describing a discipline style is difficult. In general, however, individuals' overall responses tend to fall into one of the following three main camps. (Note: It's important to be aware that these are broad-brush descriptions. Although most parents tend to tilt in one of these directions, it's often possible to find a little bit of all these three types in each of us.)

1. *The Lenient Camp.* This type of parent prefers to tread gently, rather than firmly. He's nonconfrontational, and doesn't like to make waves. He tends to indulge his child in order to make childhood a carefree safe haven. He wants his children to be happy and free to explore without being hampered by restrictions or responsibilities. Often such parents had more domineering parents themselves and are determined not to repeat that style with their own child. Above all, the lenient parent wants his child to see him as a friend.

2. *The Autocratic Camp.* This style is the polar opposite of leniency. An autocratic parent is motivated by control at almost all costs. As a result, she may lack patience and spontaneity. She dislikes deviations from what's expected, although her expectations may not always be realistic for a child's developmental stage. She tends to be inflexible regarding rules and consequences. Popular phrases that reflect this attitude: "Because I said so!" and "It's my way or else!" Such parents often had autocratic parents themselves, providing their only model for how to interact with a child.

CHECKLIST
Parents' Top Discipline Mistakes

What does it mean to be "too tough" or "too easy"? The following characteristics are associated with a bumpier road to a well-behaved child:

✔ **Lack of firmness:** Not having clearly defined rules and expectations.

✔ **Uncertainty:** Backing off or capitulating if the child doesn't comply.

✔ **Inconsistency:** Not enforcing rules and expectations regularly.

✔ **Being overly critical:** Giving attention only to point out faults.

✔ **Disrespect:** Failing to regard the child's feelings.

✔ **Laxness:** Not creating predictable household routines that foster security.

✔ **Insecurity:** Lacking self-confidence; over-reliance on tricks or parenting programs that promise unrealistic results in "three easy steps"; not trusting instincts.

✔ **Lacking patience:** Succumbing to the heat of the moment.

3. *The Authoritative Camp.* This style combines love with limits. An authoritative parent understands the importance of setting rules and enforcing them, but does so in a positive way. He creates a supportive environment in which kids feel loved, free, and trusted, yet also imposes responsibilities and realistic expectations that help his child develop the ultimate prize: self-discipline. He is not afraid to be the authority figure in his child's life.

All three discipline styles usually mean well. Unfortunately, they don't always achieve the same results. Parents who are overly lenient tend to have children who are more spoiled and self-centered. Parents who are overly autocratic tend to have children who are either unsure of themselves or openly rebellious. Providing a child with hearty doses of both love and limits—the third model—tends to yield the most successful results: a child who understands what's expected and is willing to meet you halfway, or better.

When Parents Disagree

Inevitably, you and your partner won't see eye-to-eye on the best way to handle a given situation. Usually the disconnect becomes obvious while one

CHECKLIST

Whatever Your Style May Be ...

5 Things Even Strict Parents Should Do

✔ Treat your child with respect.

✔ Make exceptions to rules sometimes.

✔ Use praise and positive reinforcement.

✔ Have fun with your child.

✔ Give lots of hugs and kisses.

5 Things Even Lenient Parents Should Do

✔ Have firm limits.

✔ Enforce rules consistently.

✔ Have reasonable expectations.

✔ Provide opportunities for developing responsibility.

✔ Let your child fail sometimes.

parent is in the middle of dealing with a problem. The other parent speaks up in a way that undermines his or her partner, dilutes the message of the moment, and confuses or even unnerves the child. So what's the best way to proceed when you feel your partner is being too lenient, too harsh, or just plain *wrong*?

- **Cool down.** Avoid hashing out your differences in the heat of the moment. Don't take a split in your parenting styles personally. Let the parent who has begun to handle the situation finish, even if you disagree vehemently. Speaking up in the middle of things undermines your partner's authority, which is detrimental to the disciplinary lesson at hand and, what's worse, will only aggravate your partner. Wait until you're able to talk it through in a calm manner.

- **Keep your child out of it.** Never argue about discipline in front of your child. Seeing parents bicker because of something he did can make a child feel frightened and guilty. He may think that he's the cause of the argument (as opposed to only being its indirect cause). Also, a child who senses discord between his parents is also more liable to manipulate the situation, or others like it, for his own benefit.

- **Stay neutral and stay constructive.** Avoid using phrases like, "You should have . . ." or "That's not the way to do it" when discussing the problem with your partner. An accusatory tone will only inflame your partner's temper (and sense of pride). Keep your focus on the strategy, not on your partner. One way to respond to something you disapprove of is to say *after* the fact, "This is what I do in that situation, and here's why it usually works." Also, limit your discussion to a specific issue ("You let Tom watch too much TV") rather than generalizing it ("You always undermine my authority").

- **Talk about the "whys."** Explain to one another how you best feel a situation should be handled and why it's important to you that it be handled that way. A parent who is annoyed by thumb sucking, for example, might feel that it's a bad habit that will result in pricy orthodontia down the road. By talking it through, though, the parent may come to realize that many two-year-olds suck their thumbs, and the habit is nothing to worry about right now. Couples especially should spend time talking with one another about how they were raised, and what they both liked and disliked about their own parents' styles of handling them.

- **Make a reality check.** A common scenario is for the parent who spends less time with the child to criticize his or her partner's responses. Example: You take your child to a grown-up party but she's wound up. She asks to go to the bathroom six times, interrupts grown-ups, takes a single bite out of many hors d'oeuvres and then returns them to the tray. "Let's go," snaps Dad. "We shouldn't have brought her here in the first place." But Mom is not nearly so exasperated. She counters, "Well, what do you expect? She's only three." The problem here is that Dad may be slightly out of tune with what's realistic behavior for a child this age.

  One solution is for the partner who's a bit out of touch to try to spend more time with his child, especially in social situations. He could spend a morning at her preschool, escort her to a birthday party, or take her to story-time at the local bookstore. By seeing his child and her peers in action, he'll gain a better sense of what's normal behavior for kids of that age.

- **Share the job.** In relationships where one parent tends to be more strict and more rule-oriented, while the other is more laissez-faire, the temptation can be great for the strict parent to handle all the problems. But this isn't fair to either parent or to the children. The stricter parent winds up playing the heavy relentlessly, either because the laid-back parent abdicates his or her responsibility to discipline or because the stricter parent never gives the partner a chance. The more easygoing parent becomes chronically undermined. He, too, needs to deal with the child, and in his own way.

In general, the parent who is in the middle of the action should be the one who handles things. If mellow Dad is playing with the kids in the evening and run-a-tight-ship Mom finds herself growing exasperated because they aren't getting ready for bed on time, they need to agree who's in charge here: Is Dad going to put the children to bed? If so, then she cedes the responsibility for the job to him and lets him handle it in his own way. At the same time, it would be the Dad's responsibility to make sure that he's generally adhering to agreed-upon house rules. For example, he might wind up putting the kids to bed a half-hour late but shouldn't let them stay up until midnight if the usual bedtime is eight o'clock. That would wreak havoc on the children's schedule and possibly penalize the mother as well if she's the one who gets the children up, dressed, and off to day care in the morning.

If you are the parent who finds yourself handling the lion's share of discipline even when your partner is around, it's a good idea to examine why this is the case. Is your spouse too passive? Are you

WHAT IF...

I want my child to think of me more as a friend than as an authority figure?

Every parent and child should aim to get along well, have fun together, talk openly, and genuinely like one another. That sort of relationship is a natural byproduct of a close parent-child relationship, and should be both cultivated and coveted. That's not the same as being your child's pal, though. It's impossible to have an equal relationship—at least until your child is well into adulthood. A parent is, by definition, an authority figure. Your child's healthy development *depends* on that imbalance of power. You know things—about your income, perhaps, or your marriage—that should not be your child's business. Your child cannot be your confidant the way your best friend might be. Nor is it in your child's developmental interest to turn to his parents, rather than his peers, for certain kinds of camaraderie and feedback. The ideal is for a child to think of you as both a friend *and* an authority figure.

too quick to step in, perhaps because you don't think your partner will handle things the "right" way or because he doesn't spend as much time with your child as you do? Discuss the dilemma. Find ways to step back, even if it means leaving the room so that your partner can handle a situation solo. It's to everyone's benefit when both parents are active disciplinarians.

- **Remember that you're both seeking the same result.** It's easy to fall into the trap of feeling you have to "win" an argument with your spouse. Or to rationalize that if "She's right, then I must be wrong." Ultimately, however, when it comes to discipline, the only winner or loser is your child. You both want the best for him—to teach him how to be a responsible, respectful, well-behaved individual. The only difference is in how to get there.

  There's no one correct way to handle a given situation. If, for example, your five-year-old leaves his bicycle outside in the rain yet again, you might say that he can't ride it for a full week. Your partner, realizing that your son will miss the big bicycle race at the playground this weekend, feels the punishment is too severe. Compromise is the key to many a discipline impasse. Perhaps your son could be grounded from bike-riding until the race, and have to complete some other task as well that reinforces the idea of responsibility.

  For other situations, you might agree to try one parent's approach, with the understanding that if it doesn't seem to work, you'll try something else. For example, if your child is using back talk, and you think reprimands are the right course of action, you might agree that if continued reprimands do nothing to curb the behavior, you will next resort to trying time-outs, your partner's suggestion.

- **Seek outside opinions.** If you're at an impasse, consider soliciting others' opinions. By talking to other parents or relatives, you might discover an alternative that neither of you had considered. Or one parent may realize that her perspective is well outside the norm of what most people would do. For couples who are really stuck, either about a specific issue or a general approach to discipline, it may be useful to talk to a family counselor as a neutral third party.

WHAT IF...

Our child's grandparents allow different standards of behavior than we do?

Grandparents are often more permissive than parents. Ask yourself how significant the differences really are: Do they indulge your child in more sweets, soda, and toys than you do? Let your child stay up later than you'd prefer? Permit shoes on the furniture? Occasional lapses from your established behavioral norms aren't going to hurt your child. Kids quickly understand that Grandma allows certain behaviors that Mom does not, and they can learn to follow both standards. This is also true if your parents' household is more strict than your own.

In fact, your standards don't need to be identical even if your parents are also regular caregivers for your child. In that event, though, you'll want to make sure that you're in agreement on certain big issues, such as the use of corporal punishment, time-outs, and daily routines. Make your preferences known, but give your parents a fair amount of leeway.

• **Agree to disagree.** Face it, you're two different people. It's a rare couple who absolutely agrees on everything in life. You shouldn't always expect to present a united front to your child. Disagreements are part of life. It's also instructive for a child to see that there are different viewpoints about certain situations. Say that you insist that your child bathe and brush her teeth before storytime at night, but when Dad is putting him to bed, toothbrushing can wait and baths are sometimes ignored completely. In the larger scheme of things, that's a benign difference of opinion. Explain to your child that Mom and Dad have different ideas about the way they like to run bedtime. A preschooler or older child is capable of accepting these two ways of doing things. Just don't get into an argument over your disagreement in front of your child.

Also remember that there's usually more than one good way to respond to a situation. Don't get hung up on procedures. A tantrum on the floor at bedtime may warrant a milder response than a tantrum that involves drawing with Magic Marker on a closet door because you said no to another video. Or if one parent has been away on a trip, on his return you might overlook a bit of your child's excitement—and wildness—that would be frowned upon under more ordinary circumstances.

It's useful to agree, in advance, about certain things that are above compromise. Especially about significant issues, both parents should have a united point of view. Otherwise you'll find yourselves having the same argument over and over. Hash out a joint perspective about such overarching issues as education, religious upbringing, corporal punishment, and household routines. It's helpful to your child to have consistent house rules about things such as unacceptable language and antisocial behavior (biting, hitting), as well as predictable consequences for breaking those rules.

WHAT WE DO
"Our Parenting Styles Clash"

"I'm such a softy. They just have to give me that look," says Mike Jackson of his two preschool-age daughters, Carey and Judy, when they've done something wrong. "I just think, 'Don't look at me that way,' but I have to step outside myself and not fall for it. It's so hard sometimes. My wife, Susan, says I let them walk all over me."

Mike and Susan approach discipline with different attitudes. Mike minds the girls until 12:30 P.M. during the week. During that time they eat breakfast and play. Sometimes Mike gives them a bath before they head off to the sitter's for the afternoon. He tends to ignore minor acting up and gives the girls brief time-outs if they hit one another or refuse to pick up a mess. Mostly, though, Mike says he prefers to talk through problems.

"I'm more lenient, though, about things that don't cause the girls or others harm," Mike admits. Susan, who generally supervises the girls from 6 P.M. to bedtime, tends to keep them on a more predictable schedule, whereas Mike for example, would let them stay up later if they wanted to. Mike lets them eat ice cream out of the container, whereas his wife insists on using bowls. "They know when they push Susan too much, they'll get spanked," Mike says.

As a result of their parents' different styles, the girls tend to run to Daddy for help when Mom is doing the disciplining. "It's hard when your child puts you against your spouse," Mike acknowledges. Once the girls wrote with markers all over their mom's journal. "I came home to take the girls to the park, and Judy ran up to me and said, 'Please hold me!' I didn't know why my wife was upset, but had to explain to Judy that since Mom had already started handling the problem, she had to go back and finish listening to her, and learn that her actions will cause reactions. So I didn't end up taking them to the park."

Mike's tips about implementing different discipline approaches:

- **Don't argue with your spouse about discipline in front of the kids.** "Whoever initiates the discipline should follow through. If my wife comes into the middle of a situation and she disagrees with what I'm doing, I'll pull her aside and explain, 'This is what I'm trying to do.' That way she'll understand where I'm coming from."

- **Stick with one discipline style.** "At least try to always be consistent with yourself."

- **Deal with it, don't ignore it.** "When the girls come to me, they think they're getting off the hook. You can't let them hide behind you."

- **Be flexible.** "Respect one another's differences. One discipline style won't work for every situation."

Why Parents Lose Their Cool

Patience is a primary virtue when it comes to raising children. When parents deal with their children in a calm, rational manner, things usually go far more smoothly. Children listen better. Parents are better able to respond appropriately. Situations don't spiral out of control. So why is patience a quality that's so often in low supply?

HOW TO

The Mommy Time-Out

Parents need time-outs too. The reason: Disciplining a child is hard work. Here's how to take a break before *you* lose it:

The short version: In the heat of the moment—just before you're about to shout, slap, or order the perpetrator to his room—remove yourself from the situation instead. Go to the bathroom and lock yourself in. Ignore the cries or poundings on the door. Count to ten. Take a deep breath and exhale. Do it again. Sometimes by taking a time-out yourself, you can recharge your emotional batteries just enough to better handle the punishment that your child deserves.

The long version: Every parent needs to make time for himself or herself during the day. You need to be able to gather your wits, to hear yourself think. You deserve a chance to be a person, not just a mom or dad. By focusing solely on yourself for even a few minutes a day, you'll be better equipped to deal with the relentlessness that is parenthood. Parents of toddlers need as much as an hour or two a day away, because safety considerations and the child's sheer energy level make refueling all the more essential. Stay-at-home parents, obviously, are particularly vulnerable.

Ideally, these getaways truly allow you to get away from your child. You might take time for an exercise class, for example, or a long walk while your neighbor babysits (and then you can return the favor while she exercises). For some stay-at-home parents, part-time work is the answer, or participation in a class or volunteer program. When it's not possible to physically remove yourself, you still need to carve out time alone. Resist the temptation to do chores while your child naps, and do something nice just for you instead. Maybe your salvation is quiet reading or writing, or a craft or hobby (scrapbook-making, knitting, woodworking—whatever tickles your fancy).

The old cliche is true: *Before you can take care of your child, you've got to take care of yourself.* (If you don't, who will?)

Because we're humans, not saints. Parents have schedules to keep, households to run, and everyday annoyances to deal with, from traffic jams to broken dishwashers. Not to mention maintaining their own health and sanity. All that, plus keeping a child on track. It's a rare bird who can greet every tantrum with a benevolent smile and handle being ignored by a defiant child without openly seething.

If you have more than one child, patience becomes an even tougher mindset

CHECKLIST
Need to Let Off Steam?

Try these pick-me-ups:

- ✔ Make yourself a steaming cup of coffee or tea.
- ✔ Take a bath.
- ✔ Call someone (preferably someone who has kids).
- ✔ Peruse some catalogs.
- ✔ Let off steam to your online mothers' support group.
- ✔ Nap when your child naps.
- ✔ Eat chocolate.
- ✔ Take a walk.
- ✔ Do twenty-five sit-ups.
- ✔ Put on your favorite CD.
- ✔ Take the kids for a walk or a bike ride.
- ✔ Bake banana bread.
- ✔ Watch mindless TV game shows or soap operas.
- ✔ Sign up for a class or join a sports team.
- ✔ Make pink lemonade.
- ✔ Pluck your eyebrows.
- ✔ Meet a friend in the park or a coffee shop.
- ✔ Practice Lamaze breathing. (Even if it didn't work in labor, it can now!)

WHAT IF...

Our babysitter spanks and we don't approve of it?

Everyone's parenting style is different, and that includes caregivers. While you need to allow your sitter a certain amount of independence to handle situations as she feels are best, it's also your responsibility to sketch out the parameters for her—and the use of corporal punishment is one area where all parties must be in agreement. Let her know your feelings on the subject. If she can't agree to avoid spanking your child, your only choice is to let her go as your sitter.

to maintain, because with siblings comes sibling rivalry. There's an exponential rise in opportunities for discord between the children, not to mention more bodies to discipline.

Some parents have a rougher time when their temperament is different from their child's. An outgoing mother may find it harder to drum up the patience necessary with a child who is reserved in social situations. A passive father may be driven to frustration by a very active, adventuresome child. Children who are strong-willed, whether it's because of their temperament or their developmental stage, test everyone's benevolence. Just as parents find it easier to get along with some adults than others, it only makes sense that relationships with some children run smoothly most of the time and that some parent-child bonds have more bumps. It's not that you love your child any less—but sometimes added reserves of patience are required.

Perhaps the best advice for parents who feel guilty about losing their cool is to give up any aspirations of perfection. You're not a bad parent because your children misbehave. You're not a failure because you can't always "keep them under control." Parenting is a slow process riddled with downs as well as ups. No parent, and certainly no child, is perfect. You will shout. You will snap. You will make idle threats. And you will hate yourself for doing these things. But as long as they are the exceptions, and not your only way of dealing with your child, you will be doing just fine.

Don't let anyone tell you that good disciplinarians are eternally calm and patient. That's the ideal, of course. But ideals are seldom attainable.

Better to make it your goal to be patient and loving as much as possible. Recognize that you'll lose your cool sometimes, and that that's okay. Brush up on your repertoire of discipline skills to keep the balance of your responses positive. And be sure that you allow yourself opportunities to recharge as well.

You can probably sense when you're on the edge. Maybe you have difficulty focusing. You find yourself sighing a lot at your child's endless demands. The familiar throb of a tension headache sets in. It's also common to find yourself feeling angry at your child—and then, in turn, to feel guilty for momentarily disliking the little person you adore. These reactions are normal. Recognizing what triggers tension for you can help you take a break before a bona fide explosion occurs.

CHAPTER THREE

Starting
Out
Right

Perhaps the single most surprising thing a new parent should know about discipline is that it's almost never too early to begin. No, this doesn't mean time-outs for two-month-olds, or making a twelve-month-old sit still in a corner. Remember the true definition of discipline: to guide and teach, not to punish. Infants and toddlers depend on you to learn virtually everything. And that includes learning right from wrong. Little ones are as much in need as older children of being kept safe from harm and of developing a sense of security that will fuel all their explorations and discoveries.

Babies also benefit from age-appropriate approaches that differ slightly from those that work with older kids.

Here's a guide to the beginnings of discipline.

Why Babies Need Discipline

Whether you realize it or not, you began disciplining your child almost at birth. How? By responding to your baby's cries, feeding him when he's hungry, holding him close, and singing or talking to him. These are all ways of building a healthy bond. You're helping your child develop a sense of security. He's learning that when he is in need, you will be there. He is seeing cause and effect. He's learning trust.

Of course, the challenges grow more complicated as your child gets older. Along with fostering a sense of security, you need to begin to set limits. A newborn cries at night because he's hungry. After a baby is a few months old, however, most are physically capable of sleeping through the night—yet he may still cry. How you react to these continuing cries will make the difference between whether you have a child who learns days from nights and mealtime from sleep time, or whether you'll spend the next year or two running yourself ragged at night with a fitful sleeper. As your baby begins to reach, scoot, and crawl, it's time to take measures to keep her safe from harm.

By the second year, parents find themselves in increasingly uncharted waters. That's because your child's world is opening up now that his strength and mobility are blossoming. There are so many new things to explore. He is also discovering his personal will and is eager to test out his newfound capabilities.

Discipline in babyhood does more than help your child feel secure. It sets the stage for future social development. Your child's actions now—and more importantly, your *re*actions—shape his future behavior. Example: Your seven-month-old reaches up to pull your hair. Your reflexive response is to shriek. But instead of abandoning the behavior, your baby sees that certain actions get a dramatic rise out of you. That seems exciting to the baby, who will try to get the same reaction again. Left unchecked, voilà, a bad habit is born.

As with an older child, it's important to correct bad behaviors while promoting

DEFINITION
Age-Appropriate

Discipline is not a one-size-fits-all proposition. Parents need to have different expectations of their child depending on her age and developmental stage. *Age-appropriate* is a way to describe activities, toys, disciplinary techniques, or expectations that are right for your child's age and stage.

good ones. It's a mission laced with special challenges for parents of infants and toddlers, though. For one thing, young children lack the verbal skills of their older counterparts. You can't engage in a dialogue with a baby or toddler who can't yet talk—at least, you can't hold a back-and-forth conversation. Understanding his viewpoint and communicating yours require different tactics. Young toddlers are also notoriously irrational. They're still working out the principle of cause and effect. They're driven by impulse. Nor does a child this age have a firm grasp of such concepts as sharing, manners, or empathy—let alone personal safety. On top of everything else, a young toddler is heady with the egocentric glory of being a toddler. He's discovering that he is a person, separate from his parents, with the power to make things happen all on his own. Sometimes he feels without limits—at least, until you point them out.

DEFINITION
Terrible Twos

Contrary to popular belief, this phrase doesn't describe a clinically recognized developmental stage. True, you hear a lot about the "terrible twos," sometimes referring to the second year of life (from twelve to twenty-four months of age) and sometimes to the child aged 2 to 3. The phrase comes from the fact that toddlerhood is when most behavior problems begin. Toddlers are headstrong, curious, and relentless. Of course, they're also funny, fascinating, and delightful.

The term *terrible twos* can be a self-fulfilling prophecy. If you expect these magical years to be more bad than good, they very well may turn out that way. But if you understand the developmental reasons your child acts the way he does and adjust your expectations and your own behaviors accordingly, you are far more likely to see this span of time for the brief, precious joy that it is. Yes, it will have its terrible moments. Let's not sugarcoat the realities of life with a toddler. But "terrible"? That's a huge overstatement.

However daunting, it's still possible to discipline a child of two and under. And better yet, you have a clean slate to work with.

Problem Prevention

Because one- and two-year-olds are so malleable, a lot of discipline at this age consists of setting them up for success. How do you do this?

- **Childproof.** Create a safe haven for exploration. By removing the obvious dangers, you're also eliminating the need to constantly hover behind your child issuing warnings and "nos." That leaves her free to investigate and play.

CHECKLIST
Why Babies and Toddlers Misbehave

Before you get angry when Baby acts a certain way, put yourself in her piggy-toes. Babies and toddlers seldom try to get your goat out of spite or defiance. First run a quick reality check: Are your expectations realistic considering the circumstances and your child's developmental stage? A baby who "misbehaves" may be:

✓ **Curious.** An infant who persists in playing with the telephone buttons or grabbing the cat's tail is fascinated rather than willfully disobedient. The sound of the buttons is interesting. So is chasing the cat and feeling its fur. Babies learn through their actions and their senses. So call it "discovery by doing" instead.

✓ **Testing his power.** Especially between the ages of fourteen months and twenty-two months, a toddler is becoming aware that he is a separate person from his parents, and that his individuality carries with it a certain degree of personal power. Continuing to kick the sofa after you've asked him to stop is his way of ascertaining his limits. It's as if he's thinking, "Can I make her really mad if I do this just one more time?"

✓ **In need of attention.** A child may be bored, lonely, or just thrilled with the agitated response that he's learned he'll get by dropping his food from the high chair. To his mind, negative attention—in the form of your reprimands or fussing—is better than no attention at all.

✓ **Frustrated.** Toddlers want to do many things that they simply can't. They may have a physical limitation, such as not enough coordination to stack ten blocks perfectly. Or the limits may be imposed, as when a parent insists on holding a child's hand when she crosses the street. A tantrum is a way to channel the frustration borne of such experiences.

✓ **Tired.** Little ones need lots of naps. If you take your child on a long morning of errands past naptime, her whininess in the checkout line won't be about a coveted piece of candy. It's her way of saying "Enough!"

✓ **Hungry.** Small children need lots of refueling. When basic needs are met (including thirst, sleep, and a dry bottom), your child is much more likely to be cooperative.

Be sure to reassess the environment as your baby grows. For an eight-month-old crawler, for example, childproofing might involve removing the planters on the floor. An eighteen-month-old walker, on the other hand, may enjoy looking at the leaves and no longer be tempted to eat them, but may need to have glass objects put out of reach on higher shelves.

- **Plan ahead to avert disasters.** If you know your child is heading for a challenging situation, plan ahead. Bring along a bag of toys and diversions when visiting the home of someone who has no children. Carry books for the inevitable wait at the dentist's office. Pack snacks and juice boxes for a car trip. If you're headed to a restaurant with a picky eater or a baby who's just graduated to finger foods, pack along his own portions just in case the menu doesn't satisfy his needs. It's a good idea to be prepared even for the shortest of outings, in case of unexpected delays. Always stash some emergency snacks and toys in your child's diaper bag.

  Time outings carefully. Mornings are often best for little ones—after breakfast but well before naptime. Try to rush through six different errands at once, and you do it at your own risk. Sometimes children will weather them gracefully . . . but the more you move your child in and out of the car seat into different stops and shops, the more likely he is to eventually protest.

- **Give ample warning before transitions.** A baby will cheerfully allow you to carry her from place to place. Beginning around twelve to fifteen months of age, however, your fledgling toddler will begin to develop different ideas about what she'd like to do when. If you summarily switch off the TV or whisk her off the playground without any advance notice, she's apt to protest loudly. (Wouldn't you?) Make transitions between activities—such as leaving the park or going to day care—more smooth by giving her fair warning about what's about to happen. Put it in a time-frame she can understand: "When you go down the slide two more times, we'll go home for lunch."

- **Offer limited choices.** Getting a young child involved is often distraction enough to make her behave more appropriately. If your child is running

WHAT IF...

My toddler won't share at playgroup?

Rethink your expectations. The concept of sharing is developmentally beyond most one- and two-year-olds. You can show a child the basics. When two kids are tussling over the same toy, ask the child who has it to give it to the other "when you are finished with it." Distract the other child.

away from you in the grocery store, for example, ask her whether she'd like to sit up in the cart or help you push. When a child is balking at having his diaper changed, ask, "Do you want Mommy or Daddy to change you?" Being asked to provide input suddenly gives a child control over the situation in a nonconfrontational way. And you are spared having to shout, "Get over here!"

• **Make it fun.** Life's a game to a baby or a toddler. Make good behavior fun by turning potential hassles into play. Trying to teach toothbrushing? Initiate a contest between you and your child to see who can brush the longest. (Once you're satisfied that the brush has swished around sufficiently in your child's mouth, you can give up first.) Sing Barney's "Clean Up" song while you put toys back into the toy box together. Make a race out of getting into the car first. Pretend the freezing icicles (your fingers) are coming and your child will have to hurry to get his socks on before the ice comes to tickle his feet frozen.

• **Provide age-appropriate playthings.** Nothing frustrates a baby faster than being given a toy that's beyond his capabilities. A little bit of challenge is good. But if your child clearly is not yet ready for a certain puzzle or game, put it away for a few months. Then try again later. You want your child to be engaged and happy when she's playing, not maddened to the point of tears or tantrums.

• **Distract from disaster.** If you sense your child balking, sometimes it's best not to force the issue. She doesn't want to sit still to have her diaper changed? Give her an intriguing new object to hold and explore. Get her involved with it, talk about it, just don't say anything about the objectionable diaper change. While her attention is engaged, go ahead with the diaper. Similarly, a new walker who can't leave the VCR buttons alone will only be more attracted to them if she sees you jumping up and clucking "No, no, no" every five minutes. The next time you see her headed that way, call her name. Lure her away from the machine with an equally

WHAT WE DO
"Taking Our Toddler Out in Public"

C.J. Nash is an active, inquisitive, and independent two-year-old. "He's fairly easygoing, but he's always on the move and touching anything at his level. He always has his eyes open and looking," says his mother, Marina, who lives in Rancho Cordova, California.

To prepare C.J. for outings, Marina and her husband, Ched, talk to him about where they're going before they head out. If he starts fussing in the grocery store, she hands him something that he can be responsible for, like a roll of paper towels or a box of cereal, to keep him occupied. She also involves C.J. in what they're doing. She'll say, "Now we have to get noodles. What kind do you want?" or talk about what they're going to make for dinner with the groceries in the cart.

In a restaurant, they give him a toy—a little car or a coloring book—to play with while waiting to be served. Because he usually gets hungry before the food arrives, Marina brings along a snack that's easy to pack, such as Cheerios or cheese sticks.

Even though C.J. usually behaves fine in public, says Marina, sometimes toddlerhood gets the best of him. One night, the family went to dinner with Ched's mother, and C.J. began yelling nonstop. So Marina and Ched took turns taking him outside. "Once we walked with him a bit, he was fine, but as soon as he sat at the table, he'd start screaming again. So we took him home. When it just gets too tough, it's easier to take him home and deal with him there," Marina says.

Her tips on taking a toddler out in public:

- **If possible, enlist help.** "My husband and I try to help each other. We work as a tag team when one of us can't take it."

- **Talk it out.** "We try not to get into power struggles when C.J. is acting up. Instead we take him aside and talk. It helps to acknowledge everyone's feelings. I'll say, 'I know you're ready to go home, but we have to pay first.' "

- **Realize your toddler is just a toddler.** "It's hard to tell a two-year-old child to sit down for long periods of time. They just don't have that ability, and always want to be a part of what's going on. If we're in a mall and he wants to go see the water fountain, I let him. It's natural for toddlers to want to try different things, and C.J. is less argumentative if we allow him to touch the water and then go on."

- **Know how to read your toddler.** "If C.J. is tired or has had a hard day, we don't go out. It just sets him—and us—up for failure."

absorbing object, such as a toy telephone or toy TV remote with buttons that can be pushed and clicked to her heart's content.

- **Offer praise for a job well done.** Applaud your child when she uses the potty, drinks from a cup without spilling, or remembers to put her books back on the shelf. You'll know you're doing something right when you hear her echo back your encouraging phrases as she watches you: "Good job." "That's great!" (Or, as one little girl said to her mother in the stall at the public bathroom, "You made a wee, Mommy! I'm so proud of you!")

- **Avoid hyperstimulation.** Little ones have a lower threshold for excitement than do older children. That's why, for instance, they tend to fall apart at their own big birthday bashes. Skip wild roughhousing before bedtime. Visit stores, pizza parlors, and other venues with lots of bright sights and sounds in brief doses. Realize, too, that some children are more easily over-stimulated than others.

- **Stick to routines as best you can.** Young toddlers don't do well with meals on the fly or naps postponed. The occasional exception is fine. But too many variations can add up to stress and, in turn, cranky or otherwise not-so-fun behaviors. Try to make life as predictable as possible, even on week-ends and during vacations.

- **Respond quickly when correcting behavior.** Babies' attention spans are as fleeting as a passing fly. To make your point, you must respond immediately, whether you're redirecting your child's attention to something safer or saying no. Wait too long and your point will be lost.

Forget These Tactics

Some practices have no value when applied to a baby or a toddler and should therefore not be used. They're either inappropriate for this age group or, in some cases, ineffective at any age. (For detailed descriptions, see Chapter 5.)

- **Spanking.** Even if you see no harm in an occasional swat to impart a strong message, spanking should never be used on a child under age 2. Aside from

CHECKLIST
Handy Distracters

Keep the following items on hand when out and about with a baby or toddler in tow.

6 to 12 months
- ✓ Toys that can be gummed
- ✓ Rattles
- ✓ Infant gym that the child can lie under
- ✓ An unbreakable mirror
- ✓ Activity quilt
- ✓ An extra bottle and teething biscuits

12 to 18 months
- ✓ Any new toy or something the child hasn't seen lately
- ✓ Shape sorter
- ✓ Board books with lots of pictures of different objects
- ✓ Finger puppets
- ✓ Stacking rings or cups
- ✓ Busy boxes with mirrors, dials, and knobs
- ✓ Dry snacks in small pieces (Cheerios, animal crackers), juice box

18 to 24 months
- ✓ Thick crayons and paper
- ✓ Wood puzzles
- ✓ Dolls and action figures
- ✓ Board books
- ✓ Videos (*Teletubbies, Barney, Blue's Clues*)
- ✓ Packages of crackers and other dry snacks, juice

24 to 36 months
- ✓ Bag of small surprises
- ✓ Sticker books
- ✓ Coloring books and crayons
- ✓ Magna Doodle toy
- ✓ Play dough
- ✓ Multiple small dolls (Playmobil figures, plastic soldiers)
- ✓ Packaged crackers, string cheese, juice

the child not being able to link the severity of your action with his own behavior, injury is a risk. For more about spanking, see "Hot Topic: Spanking," page 91.

- **Yelling.** Raising your voice to a small child is frightening for him. A toddler looks to his parents for security, and it's hardly reassuring to see a parent out of control. Because babies and toddlers are so imitative, you're also modeling the idea that using a loud voice is okay. You can almost always make your point more effectively with a calm, ordinary speaking voice. Or you can modulate your voice in a slower, deeper way to give it a serious, I-mean-business tone.

- **Reasoning.** You can't talk things through with an infant or a toddler. No matter how many times you explain to an eleven-month-old that stairs are dangerous, their allure is simply too strong. In addition to the lectures, install a gate.

- **Time-outs.** This popular behavior-shaper withdraws a child from all attention in order to distract him from undesirable behavior and let him calm himself down and behave in a more acceptable way. Although it can be a useful, positive tool, it's also a fairly sophisticated technique. *Babies and toddlers are too young to understand the purpose of a time-out or to sit still the requisite amount of time to make the point.* Instead of being a cooling-off period, the time-out becomes a power struggle. That's why using time-outs too early tends to be an exercise in frustration for both parent and child. (For more on time-outs, see Chapter 5, page 88.)

Common Toddler Behaviors

A toddler can come up with plenty of ways to vex you. There's something befuddling around every bend. The following scenarios, all common among the very young, illustrate ways you can reshape behavior in a positive way. (More general behavior problems and solutions are mapped out in Chapter 6.)

- **The diaper wriggler**
  Problem: Your child tries to escape when you change his diaper.
  What to do: Use a firm tone and expression to convey your feelings: "Be still. Help Mommy change your diaper." Keep a rotating supply of interesting toys or other curiosities on hand that your child can hold and look at. Sing a song to distract him. Don't get visibly angry or roughhouse, which turns the wiggling into a game that will continue. Budding toddlers

HOT TOPIC
Shaken Baby Syndrome

Forget the old saw, "I wish I could shake some sense into you." No matter how aggravating a baby or toddler's behavior, a frustrated adult must *never* shake or push a child. Shaken baby syndrome (SBS) is a severe and potentially fatal form of head injury. It's caused by sudden, traumatic motion, such as by being shaken, thrown vigorously into the air, or hit too hard on the back.

Newborns to age 2 are at the greatest risk. The reason: Young children's neck muscles aren't fully developed and their brain tissue is very fragile. If a child is shaken, the whiplash motion causes the brain to literally jostle within the skull. This can cause brain swelling and damage, internal bleeding, mental retardation, blindness, and even death.

While frightening and practically unthinkable, it's important to remember that the vast majority of SBS cases are caused by deliberate child abuse. Still, it's important to be aware of the danger. Young children *do* cry and whine and drive their parents crazy. It's not always easy, but try to handle your child in an even-tempered manner. If you find yourself enraged beyond control, don't address the situation right away. Place your child safely in a crib or playpen until you've had a chance to calm down.

One study found that fathers and boyfriends, followed by female babysitters, are the groups most likely to cause SBS. Perhaps, it's theorized, that persons who cause SBS are less tolerant of crying, leading them to shake the child into silence. So never leave your child with someone whom you suspect of having a problem controlling his or her temper.

Seek medical care immediately if you believe that your child may have been shaken. Signs of SBS include: a stunned, glassy-eyed look; an inability to lift the head; blood pooling in the eyes; dilated pupils that don't constrict in the light; unconsciousness; or vomiting in an otherwise healthy infant. A victim may have only one of these symptoms or none at all.

sometimes like to stand up for changes. Or, avoid arguments and simply change the diaper on a lower surface (instead of a high changing table) while he's standing.

- **The food swisher**
Problem: Your child moves around the food on his tray without eating it. What to do: A certain amount of playing with food is natural for a baby. Your child may be curious about textures, and it's fun to mix different fla-

vors. But if none of the food is making it into his mouth, try diverting his attention. Offer a bite from your plate, or invite him to have a drink of milk. If efforts to engage his appetite don't work, take the tray and the food away and call it a meal. Don't expect a toddler to sit through a meal as long as grown-ups do.

- ## The grabber
Problem: Your child has grabbed a sharp pencil or other dangerous object.
What to do: Calmly ask for the object back in a no-nonsense voice. Don't grab for it unless she's in imminent danger (holding a sharp knife, for example). Snatching the pencil away only teaches your child that grabbing is okay. Nor should you run after her, or you'll just start a chase game. Think about what signals you're sending out at the same time you're trying to achieve your objective. In a normal tone of voice, offer an intriguing alternative: "Would you like to look at my colored papers?" Your child will lose interest in the first dangerous object and gladly make the exchange.

- ## The getting-dressed lollygagger
Problem: Your child refuses to let you put his pants on.
What to do: Play peek-a-boo. Get the pants around his ankles and ask, "Where are your toes?" Your child will find this funny, and poke his feet through the leg holes in order to show you. Work with your child's developmental stage. Toddlers haven't completely learned that things out of sight are still "real," which explains the attraction of peek-a-boo games. Humor also tends to be more effective than hysteria.

- ## The clothes balker
Problem: Your child refuses to wear a certain shirt.
What to do: Instead of automatically dressing a child who is opinionated about clothing, try giving choices. She may find the shirt objectionable for reasonable cause, say because the fabric is rough, the tag is scratchy, or it's

---

WHAT IF...

My toddler prefers to sit in my lap during meals; should I let her?

Some behaviors are fun, or funny, the first few times around, until they start to grate. A good general rule of thumb when deciding whether you should curb an annoying behavior or look the other way is this: If your child were ten years old, would you let her do it? While there are age-appropriate considerations to some behaviors, in general this is a useful way to guide your reactions. If you're bugged enough to be in doubt about whether to put a stop to something, you probably should.

Q&A
What Are the Benefits of Blankies?

What do teddy bears, rag dolls, favorite blankets, and other love objects have to do with discipline? Simple. These security objects (also called transitional comfort objects or "loveys") help infants and toddlers feel more secure. They function as substitute parents in a way. They can make it easier to transition between daily activities, such as play and sleeping, and ease separation from a parent. They can also help a child cope with emotions and new experiences, including frustration, anger, sadness, fatigue, or illness.

Some children never use a comfort toy, relying on an array of different objects rather than one special thing. Others use sucking their thumbs instead. Usually the preferred toy is chosen between nine and twelve months. Devotion peaks between eighteen and thirty months, and the importance of the toy diminishes during the preschool years.

Take seriously the object's significance to your child. Pack it when you go on trips, let her bring it to the grocery store or the doctor's office. A good childcare center shouldn't frown on a single security toy at this age, especially for naptime. Some parents buy a duplicate once the baby's preference for a given object becomes clear, in case it's ever lost.

too tight. Let your child pick which of two (and no more than two) shirts she prefers. You don't need to invite her opinions on everything in her life, though. To avoid option overload, only give choices regarding situations that have become contentious, such as clothing or food.

If she seems to merely be exerting toddler contrariness about getting dressed, try distraction. Hand her a toy, point to a sight out the window, or talk about where you are going that day.

- **The mess-maker**

Problem: He starts one thing and drifts to another—and another and another, leaving a stream of blocks, Duplos, books, trains, crayons, and assorted other toys in his wake.

What to do: Start by lowering your expectations. A baby or young toddler is too immature to be expected to clean up after himself before launching into a new activity. Having a toddler around means tolerating a certain amount of clutter. You can reduce the mess by putting out just a few

WHAT IF...

My child deliberately defies me?

He's not being mean-spirited. At this age, willful disobedience is called testing. Your child wants to know what happens if he does something you've just warned him not to. Unfortunately, it can take countless repetitions for your lesson to sink in. Use words ("Don't touch!") or actions (such as redirection) to reinforce your message. Persevere, and eventually you'll be rewarded with a child who knows and follows the rules.

different toys at a time. But because little ones run through activities so quickly, you'll wind up continually having to restock. Better to leave an assortment of toys at your child's disposal. If the mess really bothers you, you can stop periodically to make a game out of cleaning up together. A toddler will be happy to follow your example. Don't expect your child to do all the tidying by himself, though.

● **The buckle-up rebel**

Problem: Your child puts up a mighty struggle when it's time to get buckled into her car seat.

What to do: Try tickling your child's upper leg. He'll relax just long enough for you to get him in a seated position and buckle the belt. Distractions like songs or a special toy to hold can further relax him long enough to be strapped in securely. Especially from about twelve months to eighteen months of age, toddlers hate to be immobilized. That goes for being diapered, getting dressed, or sitting in a high chair when they're not eating. They want to be on the move. Your life will be easier if you accept this fact and keep restraints to a minimum. Of course, for safety's sake, you can't compromise about car seats.

● **The nap renegade**

Problem: Naptime comes—and goes. And your child is wide awake.

What to do: Follow a regular nap schedule. At the appointed time, go through the usual pre-nap routines and then put your child in her crib or bed, whether or not she seems sleepy. Leave a few board books or toys available for her to play with. Sometimes a child will play awhile and then drift off to sleep. If a half-hour or more goes by and your child is not only still awake, but howling in protest, she simply may not need a nap that day. It happens. Kids have wildly different sleep needs.

But if a pattern seems to be developing—your child refuses naps with increasing frequency—she may be in a nap transition. Most children drop their morning nap between twelve and eighteen months of age. A child this age needs about thirteen hours of sleep per twenty-four hours, including naps. But that's only an average. Some children require less sleep than others, a tendency that usually emerges during infancy.

CHAPTER FOUR

It's How You Say It

What you say to your child—and how you say it—plays an enormous role in shaping his or her behavior. After all, the main way parents instruct their children is by talking to them. We tell, explain, remind, praise, warn, encourage, and correct.

As you talk, bear in mind the following guidelines to effective communication with your kids:

- Follow the three Cs: Always be calm, confident, and connected.

- Accentuate the positive: Don't overlook the importance of everyday pleasantries.

- Stay on focus: Deliver messages with impact.

- Follow through: Support your words with actions.

- Remember to listen: Communication is a two-way street.

Read on for ideas about putting these concepts into action.

Follow the Three Cs

First, the basics: Your overall attitude should be one of conviction. If you don't believe in the importance and sincerity of your words, how do you expect your child to? Children respond best to messages that are level and serious, and therefore unambiguous. They can find less wiggle room than if you are tentative, emotional, or distracted.

Always be calm. This is perhaps the simplest and most important communication skill to remember. Too bad it's not as easy as it sounds. Children have an impressive array of behaviors that drive parents bonkers. There's the endless grating wail of a whine. The out-of-control shrieks of a temper tantrum. The dogged persistence of "Why? Why? Why?" When we're not infuriated by the actions we're simply worn down by the accompanying sounds.

Nevertheless, keeping your response on an even keel always produces better results than when you betray how you really feel. In the first place, a neutral tone communicates that nothing your child does or says will ruffle you. This can stop an escalating battle of wills in its tracks. You preserve the upper hand. A calm demeanor can be contagious, too. Your child is more likely to mimic your behavior.

Keeping mellow also allows you to more rationally think through the best way to handle a situation. You're able to stay above the fray and not get too emotionally entangled. Calmness helps you avoid saying something rash that would undercut your authority. Kids are quick studies. Few are going to believe an overblown threat like, "Stop screaming now or we're never coming to the playground again!"

Always be confident. Or at least, always *look* that way in your child's eyes. That means having the courage to stick to your convictions. Self-doubt is common when it comes to being a disciplinarian. You think, *Maybe she's right—I am being mean by saying no to just one more cookie.* Or as your child collapses in a fit of protest on the sofa, you think, *Why did I turn off the TV— what's the harm in another half-hour video?* In fact, there may be nothing wrong with either of those things. But *no* needs to mean no. If you have already said no, reversing yourself only shows that you are malleable. The next time you put your foot down about anything, your child is apt to sense some wiggle room, if only she howls loudly or persistently enough. Stick to your guns.

Always be connected. Be sure you have your child's attention before you start talking. Saying "Time to get your coat on" while looking directly at your child signals more urgency than if you distractedly call out those words while you are packing up a diaper bag and talking on the phone.

Don't try to talk from two feet or two rooms away. Call your child by name to get his attention. Wait until he's looking at you before you begin to talk. You can also go over to your child. Kneel down to a toddler's or preschooler's eye level. If your child is gazing away, try saying, "Look at me," or "Let me see your eyes."

Your tone of voice matters, too. Kids as young as two can understand that a parent's tone changes the meaning of his words. The phrase, "You're so silly," spoken in fun carries different weight than if it were uttered with derision. Make sure that your words, tone, and body language are all sending the same message.

Accentuate the Positive

Congratulate good behavior. You don't have to praise your child for every little action. Keep in mind, though—your directives and comments should be as much positive as corrective. However, not all praise is alike. Helpful praise is specific and behavior-driven: "Thank you for reading to your sister while I was trying to finish the laundry. It made her happy and made me happy. You've really turned into a good reader." Unhelpful praise is generic: "You're so smart." "You're a good boy." The difference is that detailed praise provides a child with useful, unambiguous feedback about her abilities.

It also helps to thank your child for complying with a request, such as cleaning up a spill or remembering to hang up her coat. Affirmative comments make a child feel good, especially when they come unexpectedly: "I like the way you read your book so quietly while I was making lunch." "You were a big helper at the grocery store." "Thanks for not interrupting while I was on the phone." Try not to exaggerate or make a big deal of your gratitude. Be matter-of-fact.

Issue gentle reminders. Reminders help nudge a child toward good behavior. These gentle, matter-of-fact statements should be timed to bring about desired actions. For example, as your child is leaving the bathtub, say, "Please remember that wet towels go in the hamper, not on the floor." Reminders can help coach a child before entering a dicey situation in which he's likely to act up. For instance, as you head into the store with your child, tell her that you expect her to ride quietly in the cart and that she won't be able to walk through the aisles.

Reminders also serve as an intermediate step before advancing to punishment. If your child brings a cup of juice into the living room and the rule is that he can't eat or drink there, give a gentle warning. Remind your child of the consequences, too: "Have your snack in the kitchen or you won't be able to have any snack at all."

Present choices. Give your child control in certain matters by allowing him to choose between two alternatives. "Do you want to put on your socks first or your shirt?" presents a win-win situation, instead of one you risk losing if you say, "Get dressed right now or we can't go." Presenting choices also helps your child learn to think for himself and to assume responsibility for his actions: "Using pot lids for cymbals is too noisy for indoors. You can either take them outside or make music with your xylophone instead."

Don't ask. Tell. Remember the old adage, "Ask a stupid question and you'll get a stupid answer"? Avoid phrasings that invite the answer "No." You'll circumvent unnecessary battles. Say, "It's time for bed," rather than, "Are you ready for bed now?" Say, "We'll leave the park after you go down the slide two more times," instead of, "Should we go home now?"

Try when/then. Kids are more motivated by the prospect of a reward than by a dire threat. Threats only teach your child not to take you seriously. Better to describe positive consequences that your child can relate to. The reward doesn't need to be a material incentive, merely the prospect of what will be accomplished by his compliance. Letting your child know what will happen next puts a positive spin on the matter at hand.

CHECKLIST
Praise That Works

Simple acknowledgments like the following encourage your child's efforts in an honest, easy way:

✔ "Good job."

✔ "I like how you pitched in even before I asked."

✔ "I knew you could do it."

✔ "You're a big helper when you do that."

✔ "I knew we could count on you."

✔ "I like how you said 'please.' "

✔ "Thanks for helping me."

✔ "I appreciate it."

"*When* you've put your train set away, *then* I will bring out the Play-Doh."
"*When* I'm finished planting these flowers, *then* I will play basketball with you."

Count to ten. This is a form of verbal warning. If your child doesn't comply with a request, say, "I'm going to count to ten, and I'd like you to do _____ by the time I hit ten or else _____ will happen." Many kids can't resist a beat-the-clock challenge. Bonus: It's an easy way for the parent to keep calm while exercising authority. Be sure to follow through with your stated consequence if your child doesn't do what he's supposed to.

Invite input. Tell a preschooler or older child, "We have a problem. How do you think we can solve it?" This shifts the dynamics from parent versus child to you and your child together versus the problem. In that more neutral light, your child is apt to be more compliant.

Say please and thank you. Model politeness in all your interactions with your child: "Please hang up your coat." "Thank you for mopping up the spilled milk."

Stay on Focus

Parents sometimes unwittingly dilute what they are trying to say, removing some of the oomph from their words. Keep your message strong and clear.

Be specific. You understand perfectly what you mean by the following phrases: "Be good." "Be nice," "Get ready for dinner." "Clean up your room." What could be clearer? Your child, however, is better apt to comply with your wishes if you provide more details. Compare this: "Get ready for dinner" versus, "Dinner's almost ready. Please turn off the TV and wash your hands."

Specific instructions are especially useful in unfamiliar situations. If you are bringing a child to his first wedding, for example, coach him about what will happen. Read books about weddings. Then, as you are about to enter the church, explain that everyone will sit and stand together at certain times. Tell your child that he must use a quiet voice, "just like in the library," and that he will not be able to get up and run around. Later, in the receiving line, tell him that he can shake the groom's hand and kiss the bride. All of these details, delivered at the appropriate time, will help steer his behavior much better than if you simply said, "Be quiet."

Remember, brief is best. Particularly with toddlers and preschoolers, use just a sentence or two to communicate your thought: "Put your bowl in the sink." "No eating grass." Even with an older child, limit your message to the essentials: "Get your coat on or you'll be late for school." "Please don't use that tone of voice. It's not polite."

Often parents unwittingly dilute their message with pile-ons. These are extra comments and phrases that make the listener lose sight of the main point and tune out the entire message. Stick to the core message and a brief description of the consequences—no more. For example, compare the following reprimands. The first is short and to the point; not so for the second: "Here is the dog's dish. You forgot to feed him." And, "You forgot to feed the dog. Can't you tell that he's hungry? How would you feel if I forgot to feed you? You've got to remember this or we'll have to get rid of the dog. You didn't remember to take your muddy shoes off before you came in the house, either, I see."

Some parents also weave in subtle put-downs when they say too much. This includes labeling a child. For example, "Don't grab toys out of other children's hands. That's mean. You're such a bully. What am I going to do with you?"

Stick to the subject at hand. Reprimand your child about neglecting to feed the dog. But if you want to teach a lesson about it, don't toss in the fact that he also neglected to do his homework yesterday and was surly at suppertime. Neither is it constructive to project into the future: "If you can't even remember to feed a dog, what kind of parent do you think you'll be?" Piling on criticisms only serves to belittle your child. He'll be more receptive to your point if you have only one to make at a time, and make it promptly.

Use "I" phrases, not "you" phrases. It's not the child who's unlikable or reprehensible, it's the behavior. Using sentences that start with "I" subtly shifts the emphasis of your displeasure from the child to the action. Instead of "You're so messy! You forgot to put your dirty clothes in the hamper again," compare, "I don't like it when you leave your dirty clothes on the floor because they make it hard to walk through your room." The former statement sounds more accusatory, putting your child on the defensive. The latter statement, in contrast, comes across as more neutral because it's a summary of your feelings and the problem. Kids like to please their parents, and are more likely to be willing to comply if it's to make you happy.

Don't overload. Make one request at a time. Young children forget or become confused when given too many directions. Wait for your child to wash her hands before you give instructions about setting the table. When the table is set, then you can talk about sitting up straight. And when she's

---

CHECKLIST
Rhyming Rules That Help Kids Learn

Rhymes and jingles are easy for kids to remember. Some examples:

- ✔ "Please say please!"
- ✔ "Fighting boys must give up their toys."
- ✔ "If you hit, you sit."
- ✔ "A fight's not right."
- ✔ "Talk back or shout, go to time-out."
- ✔ "Stop it and drop it." (to bickering siblings)

sitting up straight, you can begin discussing the evening's agenda. Don't blast all that information at her in a single stream.

Make it catchy. This approach doesn't work for every message, not even if you're Shakespeare. But you can sometimes create catch-phrases that stick in a child's memory. A classic example: "Stop, look, and listen" (before crossing the street). One mother signals time-outs by saying, "That's enough. Stop and drop."

Follow Through

Be realistic. Don't make idle or overly dramatic threats: "If you don't stop bickering I'm going to let you out of the car right here." "One more complaint and we're never going to a restaurant again." Your child won't believe them. And she might also call your bluff: "Okay, so let me out of the car." Now you've taught your child nothing about the behavior problem and unwittingly created a new battle to deal with as well.

Reward compliance. Acknowledge your child's efforts when she does what you ask or does the right thing. You needn't go overboard. Simply say thank you. Or, "Good job!" Or, "I appreciate your putting your toy away so fast." Use nonverbal reinforcements, too, such as a pat on the back or a thumbs-up signal.

HOW TO
Issue an Effective Reprimand

Try this four-part approach. Give your child:

1. The command. "No splashing in the tub."

2. An explanation. "It makes the floor slippery and dangerous."

3. The consequences: "If you keep splashing, you'll have to get out of the tub."

4. An alternative: "Here's a cup you can use to pour with."

Respond to noncompliance. When you allow yourself to be ignored, your child learns that this is an acceptable response—and he's apt to try it again and again. If you've taken the trouble to make a request or issue a warning, you've also got to follow through with it. React promptly so your message isn't diluted.

Don't harangue. It's important for a child to understand what he did wrong. This should be accomplished in a simple, straightforward conversation at the time of the transgression, though. After he's made amends, or behaved correctly, or you've made your point, it's *over*. Don't continue to berate your child all day for something that happened at eight o'clock in the morning. Avoid retelling the story of your child's "badness" to others throughout the day. Give him a clean slate.

Remember to Listen

Healthy discipline isn't only about talking. It requires being a good listener as well. Respect is a two-way street. Children who have a strong relationship with their parents recognize that their voices are being heard. They're not merely on the receiving end of rules, reminders, or orders. Their parents are interested in their child's point of view.

Children want their parents to be emotionally available in the same way that they crave their physical presence. Listening to your child helps cement the emotional bond between you.

Ways to tune in:

- **Spend one-on-one time with your child every day.** No matter how many siblings there are or how many outside pressures compete for your time, each child deserves a half-hour or more of solo time with Mom and Dad. Make it time when you can focus on one another. Having your child accompany you on errands or helping them with their homework is good, although they don't provide quite the same quality of interaction.

- **Talk about feelings.** Not to put too touchy-feely a spin on it, but your child's state of mind can help reveal his motivations. Resist the urge to get

CHECKLIST
Strike These Phrases!

We've all heard parents utter the following phrases. Perhaps you've even blurted out one or two yourself, in the heat of the moment. Unfortunately such phrases are unproductive or counterproductive, and sometimes even harmful.

What Not to Say	Here's Why	Here's What's Better
✔ "How can you be so dumb?"	Kids take labels to heart.	Describe the behavior, not the child: "The cup you poured the juice into was smaller than the amount left in the pitcher, that's why it overflowed. Here's a towel, let's clean it up."
✔ "Stop acting like a baby."	Avoid negative labels and focus on the specific behavior instead.	"You're crying because you're mad. But I can't help you until you calm down and find your words."
✔ "Why can't you be more like Mary?"	Your child is not Mary. Comparisons incite resentment and competition, not cooperation.	"You seem to be having trouble with that. Let me help you."
✔ "If you don't stop, I'll scream."	Emotional responses give the child no incentive to behave. He might like to hear you scream.	"Please stop [that behavior]."
✔ "If you loved me, you wouldn't do that."	What's love got to do with it? Appeal to your child's desire to please and problem-solve, not her guilt.	"Please stop [that behavior.]"

CONTINUED

What Not to Say	Here's Why	Here's What's Better
"I went to all this trouble and this is how you show me your appreciation?"	Again, a guilt trip. Instead of focusing on your personal sacrifices, ask why your child is acting up.	"Why are you running away instead of eating this cake? If you're not hungry I will put it away until later."
"Quit that or I'll give you something to cry about."	Threats frighten, but they don't teach.	"Please stop doing that."
"There's no reason to be afraid."	Don't discount your child's feelings—to her they are legitimate.	"Are you afraid of the thunder? It's just the noises that the clouds make. Here, hold my hand and you will feel better."
"What's wrong with you?"	This statement is vague and shaming.	"You must be angry. But you can't take your anger out on your brother."
"Oh brother—good going."	Sarcasm is belittling and destructive, not empathetic and instructive.	"It's just an accident. Let's clean it up."
"If you come with me to the bank, I'll buy you a balloon after."	Bribes tend to beget more bribes; not everything is negotiable.	"It's time to go to the bank."
"I knew I couldn't trust you."	That's saying your child is untrustworthy, a devastating blow to her confidence. If you really thought that, why did you set your child up for a fall?	"It's okay. You're not ready yet for that but we'll try again later when you're a little older."
"Why did you do that?"	Often your child doesn't know, or can't articulate her reason. Instead volunteer your observations.	"You grabbed that toy out of the baby's hands and made him cry. Can you think of a better way you could have gotten it?"

defensive when your four-year-old shouts, "I hate you!" Instead, echo back her feelings: "You sound very angry. Are you mad because you can't find your favorite doll?" This can help her put overwhelming emotions into words when she cannot. Your child's feelings are very real to her and discounting them will only make her feel worse.

- **Empathize.** Things that seem insignificant or comical to you can have epic importance to a child. Don't brush off complaints or pleas for help. It only takes a couple of minutes to kneel down and gently collect the details about why your child is sad or upset. Letting him know that you share his dismay can take the edge off of upset feelings that might spiral out of control if ignored. Put yourself in his shoes. Ask yourself, "How would I feel if I lost my blankie/had a fight with my best friend/didn't feel like going to swimming class/broke my new cherished possession?" Play back your answer to your child: "You must be very upset," or "Does that make you feel sad?"

DEFINITION
Labeling

Little pitchers have big ears. When you fall in the habit of describing your child's personality in a certain way, your words can become a self-fulfilling prophecy. Parents often unwittingly label kids in the context of discipline. Your child hears you call him "obstinate" or "sassy" or "bossy" and, because he looks up to you and believes everything you say, he figures it must be true. Unwittingly, you may begin to think of your child in this narrow way, too, exaggerating the importance of that trait to the exclusion of others. Even labels with a positive spin—"pretty," "athletic," "smart"—can limit a child's horizons.

Better to be specific about your child's temperament and attributes when describing her to others, and give it a positive spin. For example, tell a teacher that a reserved child, "likes to take her time getting used to a new situation, but I'm sure she'll warm up as the day goes along." Tell a bright child not just that he's smart, but that he's good at math and counting money, which will be helpful when he gets older and has an allowance to manage.

Take pains to see your child as a whole package of traits, skills, and gifts. Avoid boiling his entire complex personality down to a single word or two.

HOT TOPIC
Saying No

One little word. So much meaning. Its beauty is its simplicity. *No* has a forceful ring, an unequivocal meaning. For these reasons, the word *no* is a powerful behavior shaper.

Some experts believe the word should be used sparingly. It's thought that if your child hears a litany of no, no, no all day long, he'll eventually tune the word out. "No running." "No touch." "No cookies right now." "No, you can't go outside barefooted." One way to avoid saying no so often is to rephrase your comments in the positive. If your child is running in the house, you can say, "Please walk." (This also has the advantage of being more explicit, which helps your child better understand the rule.) If your child asks, "Can I have a cookie?" you can say, "Yes, you can have a cookie right after lunch."

You can also communicate the idea of "no" without actually uttering it. Use your face—a frown, a raised eyebrow—or shake your head as your child reaches for something inappropriate. Or try uttering a negative sound like, "Uh-uh-uh," as a verbal warning. With young children, you can also eliminate many of the times you'd have to say "no" by safety-proofing their play areas and making the spaces age appropriate. That automatically increases your opportunities for saying yes instead of no.

However, not everyone feels that the word *no* is a dreadful negative from which little ears should be spared. The word *no* can be a terrific tool that can—and should—be dispensed as necessary. It's certainly an effective way to communicate boundaries.

Best bet: Use *no* whenever you mean "Absolutely not." Set the limit, stick to it, and make it clear that there will be no wavering on this point.

This approach also works when your child covets something, whether it's an ice cream from a stand you've just passed on the beach or a toy car in the supermarket checkout lane. Again, play back his feelings: "You must want that car a lot." "Why do you like it so much?" "What would you do with it?" Simply acknowledging his desires is not the same as giving in to them. But it allows the child to vent and lets him know that you respect his thoughts. Rather than feeling like he's lost, the way a sharp "No" would, he instead feels satisfied. (*Caution:* This strategy is fairly useless with toddlers, who will assume from prolonged conversation that you are about to give in. Better to distract them from their desires and move on.)

CHECKLIST
Classic Lines We Find Ourselves Repeating

What parent hasn't heard some echoes from her past burble up to her lips? Bear in mind that letting off steam may make you feel better, but these phrases are rarely very effective.

- ✔ "Because I said so!"
- ✔ "Because I'm the mother, that's why."
- ✔ "Don't take that tone of voice with me!"
- ✔ "Wipe that smile off your face!"
- ✔ "Mark my words!"
- ✔ "Do what your mother says!"
- ✔ "If I've told you once, I've told you a million times . . ."
- ✔ "Are you deaf?"
- ✔ "Wait till your father gets home!"
- ✔ "This is the last time I'm telling you."
- ✔ "When you're the mother you can make up the rules."

- **Ask leading questions.** Inquire, "How was school today?" and the answer is bound to be, "Fine." Even asking, "What did you do in school today?" is too vague. ("Nothing," your child will say.) Pick up on things that you notice in the classroom, in the school news bulletin, or in your child's homework. Or ask about the rhythms of the day. "I heard you had a visitor in your class today." "Whose turn was it for show-and-tell today?" "Who did you play with at recess?"

- **Make time for conversation at bedtime.** Some of the best conversations with young children can occur when you're tucking them in. The whirl of the day is over and the coziness of the blankets (and your presence) invites some kids to turn reflective, so try not to rush through your bedtime ritual. Make open-ended statements like, "We had a busy day, didn't we?" Or recap some of the day's highlights together. Your child may ask about something that puzzled him earlier, such as "Why did that lady in the park have crutches?" Or he may ask something that's been percolating in the back of his mind, like "Why is the sky blue?"

- **Talk in the car.** As kids get older, they often grow less forthcoming in direct conversations, even though they're still bursting with things to tell you. For some kids, driving in the car is a great place to connect with Mom or Dad. The lack of direct eye contact helps them feel more comfortable opening up.

CHAPTER FIVE

Tactics That Work

Every parent develops his or her own storehouse of strategies for guiding a child's behavior. Some are preventative, gently steering your child to a desired outcome. Others are more punitive, applied in response to an action. Neither type is necessarily better than another. Effective discipline takes a mix of preventative and punitive measures. That's because no single tactic is useful in every situation. Nor does the same situation always merit the exact same response.

For example, you might choose one of a dozen different ways to handle a defiant child who's refusing to do something. Is he a toddler or a kindergartner? Is he refusing to stop pinching his sister, or refusing to eat any lunch? Are you at home or in public? Is it a holiday or an ordinary day? Is it early or late in the day? Each of these conditions influences your response.

Nine Terrific Tactics

This chapter explains some of the most common discipline techniques. Unlike the broader tools outlined in Chapter 1, such as modeling good behavior yourself and setting limits, these techniques are more specific. (A guide to common behavior problems and how to handle them follows in Chapter 6.) They're discussed in order, roughly from the most positive and preventative to the more punitive.

The top nine tactics for children ages 6 and under are as follows:

1. *Positive reinforcement:* Giving your child feedback when things are going well, so that you're not exclusively focusing on poor behavior.

2. *Selective ignoring:* Deciding which infractions are worth intervening over in the first place.

3. *Redirection:* Distracting a child from inappropriate behavior and channeling his energy to a more acceptable activity.

4. *Reminders:* Verbally intervening with warnings and reminders before trouble strikes.

5. *Reasoning:* Using explanations to steer behavior.

6. *Natural consequences:* Letting a child experience the natural fallout of his actions.

7. *Logical consequences:* Letting a child experience consequences that you have devised and that are related to the situation.

8. *Withdrawal of attention:* Taking away the thing your child craves most: attention from you.

9. *Time-out:* A specific method of removing your attention.

1. Positive Reinforcement

Also called positive discipline, praise, catching your child being good.

What it is: Accentuating the positive, giving encouraging feedback, praising your child for something done well. This tactic includes setting a good example and modeling the sort of behavior you expect.

What ages it works best with: All ages.

How to use it: Most simply, this tactic works by providing a loving environment in which you set your child up for success. Give your time and attention to him. Encourage your child's efforts. Let your child know by your own actions and words what you expect of him.

Use praise, but do so judiciously. If you praise too often and about every little thing, your words risk ringing hollow. Positive reinforcement is best applied in a specific way to a specific action: "I like the way you put all the Legos back into the box." "You were thoughtful to give the baby her blanket." "Thank you for remembering to say please." These statements give your child concrete feedback about an action. That sends a stronger message than if you dole out blander compliments such as "You're so smart," or "Good girl."

You can also reward your child in subtle ways, such as giving her a thumbs-up when you see her putting her blocks away, or affectionately tousling her hair for giving a visiting Grandma a kiss without being prompted. Nonmaterial items, such as hugs and compliments, are generally more effective than material rewards. If you promise your child a Beanie Baby for every time she makes her bed, the focus shifts from the value of a job well done to the acquisition of the prize. Ultimately, this is less gratifying to the child, and you're left with a potential problem once you decide that her room is crawling with so many stuffed critters that you're not going to buy any more.

Why it works: Children crave parental approval. Your feedback begets more good behavior because it has given your child positive feelings about being compliant.

2. Selective Ignoring

Also called picking your battles, letting the little things go.

What it is: Not all misdeeds are alike. Selective ignoring means deciding whether a child's problematic behavior is worth getting involved in, and letting pass without comment what's not.

What ages it works best with: All ages.

How to use it: Most parents develop a priority list for active discipline. There are certain points on which you'll want to stand firm no matter what: Everyone must wear their seat belts or be strapped in a car seat. No running with scissors. No hitting, ever. But the vast majority of situations fall into a gray zone. For these you must decide whether you'll step in or look the other way. Generally, if a situation doesn't hurt anyone or anything and doesn't set a dangerous or hurtful precedent, it can often be ignored.

Ask yourself, is this worth making a fuss over? What if your three-year-old wants to wear a striped shirt, a polka-dot skirt, and blue jeans to preschool? You may feel that it reflects badly on your own fashion sense, but is there any serious harm in it? Or say your son refuses to wear his hat in the winter. It's his head, after all. If he gets cold, he'll probably put it on—unless you've made such a big deal about the hat that he stubbornly refuses (lest he lose the power struggle that has been set up). What about a four-year-old who begins to eat her milk-sopped cereal with her fingers, rather than a spoon? She's not hurting anybody, but neither is she exhibiting the good table manners that you know she's capable of and would prefer she demonstrate in the future. In that instance, you might decide that intervention is important. Give her the choice of using her spoon, or of having the cereal taken away. Say something like, "You must be finished, since you are only playing with it."

With older children, you can encourage them to try to solve certain problems on their own. To siblings bickering over the comic pages in the paper, for example, you might say, "You're big enough to try to work this out. If you can't, I'll put the paper away."

Why it works: Selectively ignoring certain situations gives your child a measure of independence to try to do things on her own and in turn to learn on her own. And the benefit for you is that by not turning insignificant issues into big ones, you spare yourself a great deal of grief. Parents often unwittingly become engaged in power struggles when they make mountains out of molehills.

3. Redirection
Also called distraction or changing the scenery.

What it is: Beautiful in its simplicity, redirection simply means diverting a child from potential problems, usually by casually substituting another activity for the current one.

What ages it works best with: From early infancy on; ideal for babies, toddlers, and preschoolers.

How to use it: If your child is banging on a table with a toy hammer, give her a dust cloth and show her how to wipe the tabletop instead. If your child persists in asking for a cookie right before dinner, you could engage her attention in something else: "Let's look at this new library book I got for you today while we wait for dinner."

Sometimes the solution is to completely change the scene, such as going outside if your child has begun to get restless indoors, or putting on a short video after a bout of floor play begins to turn to roughhousing. You can also use redirection to teach your child a more desirable alternative. If she is trying to grab the dog, you can show her a gentler way to pet him between the ears. Or you could model more appropriate behavior for her with a toy dog.

Even your voice alone is enough to distract a young child. Try calling out his name. You don't have to use a challenging, warning tone; simply saying, "Aaron, come here!" might be intriguing enough to make the child forget his target.

Humor is another effective way to distract. If your child is whining in her car seat about being tired of sitting, ask if she can see the monkeys in the treetops. Or start singing songs or saying nursery rhymes with mixed-up words: "Humpty Dumpty sat on a wall. Humpty Dumpty had a great fall. All the king's horses and all the king's men ate scrambled eggs for breakfast again."

Why it works: Young children have short attention spans. Even if they grow fixated on something, the lure of a novel experience or merely a change of pace is usually enough to make them forget the first thing they were going after. Redirection lets you avoid chastising or making a scene while initiating a better alternative for your child.

4. Reminders
Also called verbal redirection.

What it is: Reminding your child of rules or expected behaviors and sometimes warning in advance about the consequences.

What ages it works best with: Toddlers and up.

How to use it: Issue a gentle reminder just before your child will need it. Say, "Remember to flush," as he goes into the bathroom. Warn a child who's prone to biting that such behavior is not allowed at day care while you're walking out of the house to the car. Use reminders to reinforce a rule: "Wash your hands before dinner."

A reminder is more subtle and therefore more likely to produce results than an order. There's a small but important distinction between the two: Orders tend to be barked, command style, and often come out of the blue. Reminders should be uttered matter-of-factly, restating what your child already knows. It should be a positive interaction, designed to help your child achieve a desired objective. No need to use a menacing, ominous, "Do this *or else*!" tone. That's a threat.

A warning can also include a brief "why" statement: "We don't hit. If you hit, you'll have to go to time-out." "Don't forget to put your dirty uniform in the hamper, or it won't be clean for soccer tomorrow."

Why it works: Frustrating though it is for parents, kids need to hear things again and again before the lesson is absorbed. They not only have short memories (about some things, anyway) but they're constantly processing new information. Something you said yesterday about hanging up a coat is liable to be totally forgotten in today's hubbub of coming in the door, anticipating a snack, showing you the new sticks he's picked up, and so on. By giving a reminder—"Hang up your coat, please"—you're arming your child for a successful outcome. These may seem like small things to say, but they can have a big effect on your child's behavior. As a result, you also spare yourself a certain amount of nagging and punishing. To put yourself in your child's shoes, think back to learning a new card game for the first time. You probably needed to have the rules and regulations whispered to you repeatedly, until you caught on.

5. Reasoning
Also called talking it out.

What it is: Explaining your viewpoint—why you have a particular rule and why you expect your child to abide by it.

What ages it works best with: Kindergarteners and up. A child must have good verbal skills and the ability to reason before this tactic has much merit.

How to use it: Reasoning happens naturally in a healthy relationship between parent and child. You probably explain things to your child all the time. She asks questions; you answer. Reasoning is an extension of this kind of back-and-forth conversation, focusing on behavior. Often words alone can point out the correct path to take. For example, if your child has taken a carving knife from a drawer to open a package, you can tell him, "Please put that knife down. You're not allowed to use those knives because they are so sharp. It might slip and cut your hand badly, even if you are being very careful." With a younger child, you'd just remove the knife and say, "No touching. Sharp." (Or better still, safeguard the drawer so the child can't get into it.) An older child can respond to more information, and will probably retain the lesson better as a result.

It's crucial to know how *not* to use reasoning. It's futile to attempt to reason with a toddler or young preschooler, for instance, because they are not fully rational creatures. Because of their stage of development they are more motivated by a need for immediate gratification and the drive to exert their own will than they are by logic. It's also easy to overuse reasoning with an older child or to use it in situations where it's not warranted. If you talk too much, even in a kindly and reasoning way, you will be tuned out. Better to keep your conversation to the point. Sometimes parents mistake reasoning for pleading. A child can easily manipulate a parent whose first impulse is just to cajole and beg: "C'mon, Sammy. You know you can't run away from me in the store. Don't you want to come hold my

CHECKLIST
Common Time-Out Mistakes

It's got a catchy name and a good reputation, so parents often mistakenly use time-out as the ultimate solution for all their child's disciplinary problems. Not a good idea. Time-outs have valuable—but *limited*—usefulness. Take care not to fall into these traps:

✔ **Overreliance on time-out.** Firmness is great. But if you invoke a time-out for every little infraction, you'll soon have an escalating battle of wills on your hands. The focus shifts from the child's actions to you and how "mean" you are. You've diluted the power of this tool. Better to limit time-out to three or four serious misdoings, such as hitting or talking back. For other things, develop a repertoire of alternative responses. It helps to think of time-out not as punishment per se, but as a teaching tool—a way to let your child collect his wits and reflect on his conscience. And, hopefully, a way to learn to better control himself next time.

✔ **Beginning time-outs too soon.** They won't work before a child is developmentally capable of controlling his impulses or connecting his actions with your response. Around eighteen months of age, you can introduce the idea by holding a child firmly in your arms for a couple of minutes following antisocial behavior, such as hitting or biting. But don't expect her to understand yet. Childproofing and redirection are more effective tactics for babies and toddlers. You'll have better success if you wait until your child is at least three, or even four, before you begin. A child needs to have developed some sense of reason.

✔ **Applying time-out inconsistently.** Don't call a time-out for pushing today, then ignore it tomorrow. And try not to use it for both gross infractions and minor irritations alike. Decide which behaviors merit time-outs and stick to this plan.

✔ **Acting too belatedly.** The time to invoke time-out is immediately after the misbehavior occurs (or is escalating wildly). Don't wait until you feel more up to it

hand? Please? If you run ahead, you might get lost—hey, Sammy, come back here." Talk alone cannot guide a child's behavior. When misbehavior is persistent, hurtful, or deliberately defiant, you'll need to back up your words with actions, such as removing him from the situation or placing him in a time-out.

Why it works: Reasoning is effective when used correctly because it treats a or can find a more convenient moment. Never threaten a time-out "when we get home." The best time to impart your message, especially to a young child with a short memory, is immediately after the misdeed.

✓ **Showing too much emotion.** Keep your reactions brief and blasé. Don't argue. Don't harangue. And never lose your cool. Remember the whole idea is for time-out to be neutral and uninteresting. A general discipline guideline is this: Be engaging when your child is good and boring when he's bad, even if you're furious.

✓ **Attempting to soften the blow.** Don't pity your little rule-breaker after the fact and offer kisses and cuddles. Skip contrite statements like, "I'm so sorry I had to put you in time-out but kicking is naughty so please don't do it anymore, okay?" Doing these things is still providing positive feedback for a negative behavior, which is counterproductive. After a time-out is over, forget about it. You might issue a terse reminder, like "Remember, no kicking." Then don't say or do anything more.

✓ **Making it last too long.** The minute-per-year rule is a good *maximum* amount, not a minimum. If a child is sent to a time-out for fifteen minutes, an hour, or an afternoon, you can be sure he will have forgotten the purpose of the time-out. Instead of calming down, he'll become resentful and angry at you. That's not the point of a time-out.

✓ **Expecting immediate results.** Kids who are new to time-outs sometimes act worse before they improve. The reason: Self-discipline is only learned gradually.

✓ **Thinking that time-out is a miracle cure.** Time-out is just one of a whole constellation of disciplinary tools that parents can choose from. It's not a cure-all for any disciplinary problem. Many parents choose not to use time-outs at all, preferring to rely instead on other, less punitive tactics.

child with respect. It talks neither up nor down to the child. It invites him to be an active participant in shaping his behavior.

6. Natural Consequences

Also called learning from one's mistakes.

What it is: Letting the child experience the natural aftereffects of his choices.

What ages it works best with: Preschoolers and up.

How to use it: Let your child know what will happen if a certain behavior persists, and give her the opportunity to decide what happens next. "If you keep sneaking all that candy off the party trays, you'll get sick." Consequence: The child slows her candy consumption, or continues nibbling and gets a stomachache. "You need to get in the car now, or we'll be late for preschool." The child takes her seat and makes it in time for the morning circle time, which she loves, or continues to delay and misses circle time that day. "You might not want to take that doll to the playground because she will get dirty." The child leaves the doll safely at home, or takes it to the playground, where she either looks after it, or lets it get dirty or possibly lost.

Resist the temptation to scold or say, "See, I told you so" afterward. Experiencing the consequences is a learning lesson in itself for your child. Saying more only rubs salt into the wound and isn't necessary.

Why it works: Natural consequences allow your child to clearly connect her decisions with subsequent actions. She learns an indelible lesson in responsibility.

7. Logical Consequences
Also called withdrawal of privileges or taking something away.

What it is: Letting the child experience aftereffects that have been predetermined by the parent as responses for certain behaviors. These consequences should have a logical connection to the situation. Often parents remove a desired privilege or object (cancelling an outing because homework was not finished), or the child has to make amends (cleaning up a mess, paying for a broken window).

What ages it works best with: Ages 5 and up.

How to use it: Agree in advance what the guidelines for this consequence will be. The bicycle must be put away in the garage at night or it can't be ridden the next day. Homework must be finished before soccer practice, or he can't go. If two children are fighting over a toy and cannot resolve their differences, the toy is removed from play for the day. In each instance the child has a clear choice to make. This helps him learn self-management as well as what your rules are. The privilege in question must have a connection to the offense in order to make sense to the child and therefore be more effective. This is different and usually more instructive than simply issuing a generic punishment, like spanking or a time-out.

You can't always present a choice ahead of time, as it's impossible to anticipate all situations. Sometimes consequences must simply be imposed, such as in the example of a broken window. Generally, though, your child comes to learn that when she does something she's not supposed to do, there will be a swift, related consequence.

Often kids react angrily to the removal of an object or a privilege. Try to remain matter-of-fact. This preserves your authority. If you take the bait and begin a debate, it's a no-win situation for everyone.

You can also award privileges in return for specific efforts. "If you can make it through the shopping trip for school clothes without whining, complaining, or crying, I will let you pick out a comic book afterward."

Why it works: Clear consequences teach self-control because they help a child learn to make decisions: *if* I do this, then *that* will happen. When the consequences logically follow the behavior, they're more easily understood and perceived to be fair. The child also has a vested interest in complying.

8. Withdrawal of Attention

Also called isolation, ignoring, sending a child to his room.

What it is: Removing positive attention from your child when you dislike a particular behavior.

What ages it works best with: Older toddlers, around ages two and a half to three and up.

How to use it: Withdrawing your attention can take several forms. Unlike the selective ignoring tactic, in which you let minor problems pass without comment, in this case you deliberately ignore a particular behavior that is

---

WHAT IF...

We're out in public and our child needs a time-out?

All disciplinary tactics are portable, including time-out. You don't need to have a special chair to sit in. A park bench, your car, or any spot will do. Act the same way that you would at home. And never mind what passersby think.

undesirable. Say your child is whining. Tell her that you cannot talk to her until she resumes speaking in a normal tone of voice. If the whines persist, you simply ignore her. Eventually your lack of response will be so frustrating that she'll get the message and stop whining. This will require perseverance on your part. And if the whining escalates to other, worse behaviors that cannot be allowed to continue, such as hitting you with her fists, you'll need to take other action.

Another way to withdraw your attention is to physically remove the child from what he's doing. This is a loose form of time-out, discussed in detail below. Substitute being alone for being together, such as by sending the child to his room until he can cool down. Take care not to overdo it, though. If you banish a child to his room for the evening, your point about his unacceptable behavior will be lost. Instead, he'll grow angry at being isolated and may get into more mischief. And he'll be deprived of the opportunity to show you that he can do better. A form of this tactic for those you're just beginning to discipline: A toddler can be placed in a playpen or behind a gate, just out of your reach, for a few seconds to reinforce that what he was doing was wrong.

Why it works: Children crave parental interaction and approval. By showing your approval when things are going well, and removing it when they're not, you're helping the child understand the difference between desirable and undesirable behaviors.

9. Time-Out

Also called quiet time, thinking time, isolation.

What it is: Time-out is a specific form of withdrawing attention. It provides a break in the action in an unemotional way in order to teach children self-control by giving them the opportunity to change their behavior.

What ages it works best with: Ages 3 and up. For kids two and a half to four, limit its use to aggressive acts only. Don't use this tactic for those kids under age 2.

How to use it: Time-outs can be highly structured or rather flexible, depending on your preference. The basic idea is to briefly interrupt the inappropriate

HOW TO

Use Time-*In*

Time-outs have become a staple in the modern parents' reservoir of disciplinary tactics. Too often overlooked, however, is the simple concept of the time-in. In a nutshell, it means: Catch 'em being good. Show your child love and support when he's behaving well, before a problem erupts. Give hugs. Compliment a particularly tall block tower or a puzzle that was put away without a reminder. Offer a treat with no strings attached—not as a reward or a bribe.

behavior and deprive your child of a source of pleasure—your attention. Some parents designate a special chair, corner, or other place where the child must go for a specified period of time. If the child won't sit still, keep putting her back and sit there with her. Better yet, have her sit on the floor right where she is with her head down. The last thing you want to do is start chasing her into the penalty box, since the negative excitement of the chase still provides pleasurable engagement with you—and by the time she's caught, her transgression will be long forgotten.

Take care to be passive and neutral when putting your child in time-out. But always explain why you're invoking it. Say something like, "You know that kicking is not allowed. You are in time-out for kicking." Keep the focus on the behavior, not the child. Don't talk to your child during the time-out. The idea is for it to be a dull withdrawal of positive reinforcement: no talk, no TV, no toys (even comfort toys).

How long should you keep your child in time-out? One rule of thumb is to penalize the child for one minute for each year of her life (three minutes for a three-year-old, for example). Set a timer to act as the neutral party that "decides" when the punishment is over. If the child bursts into tears, some parents wait until the child has collected himself before they start the timing. Or they may add minutes for talking or fussing. Other experts feel that the length of time is not as important as seeing the desired effect—breaking the action and getting the child to calm down. You could ask a younger child to sing a song agreed on in advance. Or you could ask your child to show you when he is calm and ready to play nicely again. Some parents simply send their child to her room until she can come back and be more civilized. True, the child may find other activities to amuse her in her stimuli-filled bedroom, but this doesn't really matter. You have achieved your goal of breaking the action, and by being alone in her room, your child is also removed from your attention.

Why it works: The magic of time-out is that it's a neutral, predictable sequence of events—no shouting necessary. Its potency lies in the fact that kids want their parents' approval and attention more than anything, and dislike being pointedly deprived of it. Bonus benefit: Time-out gives Mom or Dad a chance to regain composure, too.

Parent Traps: What *Doesn't* Work

A parent trap is a bad habit. It's a less-than-ideal way of dealing with your child, and it can be either ineffective or downright damaging. Almost all parents fall into them sometimes. They tend to be born out of familiarity—it's your knee-jerk response to situation *x*, or perhaps it's the way your parents treated you. Sometimes sheer loss of control prompts these unproductive reactions. Sometimes in the stress or fatigue of the moment we just can't think of a better way. Needless to say there almost always *is* a better way. Here, is a tour of the most common bad habits parents have regarding discipline, and how to avoid them.

The Bribery Trap

Bribery is attractive to parents because it seems to work—and work astonishingly swiftly. To a clingy child, while Mom is trying to write checks: "If you just leave me alone for five minutes, I'll take you to the ice cream parlor." To a whiner, while exasperated Dad is trying to finish his errand in the shoe store: "If you're quiet while I buy these shoes, I'll let you pick out a new Barbie at the toy store." There's no doubt that bribing a child to be good scores results. What's wrong with this action plan is that it's shortsighted. Your child behaves well for the moment—long enough to win the prize—without developing a sense of self-control for self-control's sake, of being well-behaved just because that's what she's supposed to do.

Bribery also tends to escalate. Today it takes one candy bar in the checkout lane to keep your child from screaming in the grocery store. Tomorrow he'll demand a candy bar and a balloon. Where does it end? What began seeming like an innocent treat can quickly backfire into something more akin to black-

HOT TOPIC

Spanking

After a couple of decades of being publicly reviled, spanking seems to be making a comeback. The practice actually never disappeared in many households, it just didn't get talked about. Now the voices—pro and con—can both be heard loudly. Does spanking send an I-mean-business message to help keep a child in line? Or is it the ineffectual sign of a parent who's lost control?

The latest research tends to side with the spanking-isn't-effective camp. Numerous studies have shown that hitting a child is a weak deterrent to misbehavior. Although in the short term it may quickly end an undesirable behavior, it also introduces longer-lasting problems. A child who is spanked is likely to remember your physical force far longer than what he did wrong. Therefore hitting a child imparts no lasting lesson about the right way to behave, only that it's best not be caught in a misdeed. Worse, corporal punishment reinforces the idea that might makes right, that bigger people can control smaller ones by force. And because hitting is a learned behavior, kids who are struck tend to strike out at others. For all these compelling reasons, many child-rearing authorities and parents believe that spanking should never be used under any circumstances.

At the same time, there's little evidence that an occasional swat—given only rarely and always with an open hand on a clothed bottom—will cause lasting emotional damage. Nor is an occasional spank going to turn your child into a defiant delinquent later in life. No one recommends spanking a child as a primary discipline tool. But some proponents do believe that a spanking can convey a strong message when a child does something particularly dangerous, such as run into a street.

Overall, spanking is best not used, but at the least it should be used *judiciously*. Not only is the evidence of its usefulness murky, but it's too easy for a habit of spanking, begun early in a child's life, to escalate into too much, too hard. Besides, numerous proven approaches work better. (See the tactics discussed throughout this chapter for help.) Build a disciplinary repertoire with other tried-and-true tactics you can try first, such as redirection and time-out. And for safety's sake—*never* hit a child under age 2.

mail. Moreover, if he expects prizes at the grocery store, he'll begin to associate them with any outing. It may seem hard to believe, but children value your time, praise, and attention more than a collection of stuff.

What works better: Reward good behavior, rather than bad. Before you begin writing checks or head to the shoe store, outline what you expect of your child: "I need to write some checks for a few minutes. You will have to play by yourself. Why don't you work on that puzzle, and when I'm finished I can join you." Let your presence and your praise be the reward. Leave material goods out of it. The reward should be of your invention, not your child's. A child who says, "I'll go with you to the shoe store if you promise to buy me a Barbie if I'm good" is a budding extortionist. The parent picks the treats, not the child.

WHAT WE DO
"Why We Spank"

Amy Epperson doesn't use spanking as the only way to teach her three-year-old daughter, Anna, but she feels it has its place. "Anna is really headstrong and stubborn. Sometimes I have to tell her four times to stop doing something, like teasing the dog," says Amy, who lives in Bryant, Alaska. "As a last resort, I'll swat her a couple of times behind the legs."

Though she tries to keep her daughter's age and normal behaviors in perspective, she believes that a swat is sometimes the best way to get her daughter's attention. Amy's husband works out of town during the week, and she admits that the full burden of discipline sometimes gets to her. "I feel like a single mom when my husband is traveling. Anna keeps testing me and I find myself telling her things over and over again," Amy says. After a spanking, Anna must sit on the rug until she's calm, then she can return to play. "I try to talk to her after and ask her if she understands why she got a spanking, and explain what she should have done instead," Amy says. "Spanking works for us. My husband and I were both spanked when we were young, and we're both well adjusted."

More of Amy's thoughts on corporal punishment:

- **It's a matter of degree.** "I swat pretty lightly on the back of her leg with an open hand—never with something like a wooden spoon. I do it to get her attention. Beating is an entirely different thing."

- **Realize that every child is different.** "If you have a mellow child and can discipline him with just a lecture, that's great."

- **Don't hit just to let off steam; if you must hit, it should be to make a point.** "A child doesn't fully understand the difference between right and wrong just yet, and this is one other way I can teach that."

That's not to say that you should never offer things as incentives or rewards. It's fine to tell your child in advance that if he is quiet and doesn't whine during a lengthy shopping trip, you'll buy him a snack afterward. But the incentive should be a surprise or a treat, something inconsequential like food (so you don't create a gimme monster), and of your own choosing.

The Nagging Trap

"Get your coat and hat on. Don't forget your hat. Why isn't your coat on yet? You'll freeze without your coat today. Hurry up and get your coat or you'll be late." You may think that you're being helpful by keeping after your child with countless reminders before a certain task is finally done. But this is what it sounds like to your child: *"Yadda yadda yadda."* Nagging is hollow. Kids tune it out because repetitions lose their meaning. What they respond to are clearly defined responsibilities and consequences.

What works better: Rather than driving yourself crazy with endless nattering, let your child know just once or twice what's expected. For instance, on a day when the weather has been changeable, you might say, "It's cold outside today so you'll need your coat. Let's go." If your child forgets the coat, so be it. He will be cold. And he will probably not forget it the next cold day. The goal of healthy discipline is not just to groom a well-behaved child, but to teach your child how to act responsibly.

The Yelling Trap

"Stop doing that!" "Come here right now!" "Enough, already!" Shouting is a perfectly normal human response. It lets us release steam when we are at rope's end. It feels good! Alas, aside from releasing some pent-up tension in the yeller, it accomplishes next to nothing in terms of shaping a child's behavior.

In fact, chronic yelling has the negative effect of gnawing away at a child's sense of self-worth and self-confidence. It's frightening to hear. It's also scary for a child to see his parent, to whom he looks for stability, coming unglued. Nor does it do much to model self-control.

WHAT WE DO
"Why We Don't Spank"

Around age 2, Stuart Gordon began throwing tantrums as an attention-getting device. His favorite words became *no, mine,* and *go away.* He'd find the family's CDs and throw them all over the floor. When his mom, Sue Nelson, gave him a stern "No!" he'd nonchalantly head back to the CDs and make an even bigger mess. But Sue and her husband, Steve Gordon, who live in Denver, had decided against striking their only child. "It takes more work not to spank, but physical reinforcement just seems like the coward's way out," Sue says. "Sometimes spanking is nothing more than a release for a parent who's pissed off."

Instead of spanking, Sue gives her son a time-out. She tries to look at things from Stuart's perspective. "It seems unfair to hit Stuart because he's so young and not completely capable of understanding what I need him to do," Sue says. "If I spank him, the lesson I'm trying to teach him will get lost because all Stuart will think about is his sore butt."

Her other thoughts on corporal punishment:

- **Know about your child.** "I tend to read a lot about basic psychological issues. I've learned what to expect from my child and how he's going to react. Knowing this has gotten me through a lot."

- **Remove the problem before it starts.** "We have the cheapest rugs and have removed the valuable and breakable items from Stuart's reach. The placement of furniture had to be adjusted. Stuart has an amazing arm and throws things, so we've given him squishy, soft toys to alleviate the reason to cause aggravation. Then, he doesn't have the chance to earn a punishment."

- **Allow your child to be a child.** "I don't see parenting as a policing action. Stuart is charismatic and expresses creativity in how he plays. I don't want to inhibit him by spanking him when he doesn't play 'correctly.' "

- **Try positive reinforcement.** "When Stuart has a tantrum, I remove him from public view as soon as possible so the focus is just him and me. He screams for a while, and after he's done I reassure him that I still love him and explain that his behavior isn't appropriate."

- **Don't fight aggression with aggression.** "I'd ask myself, am I disciplining to make myself feel better or to make my child better understand?"

What works better: The first step to break the yelling habit is to collect yourself. Count to ten. Walk away rather than saying anything at all. Practice your Lamaze breathing. One mom implements what she calls "the invisible pediatrician rule": She tries to respond to her child the way she would if her favorite doctor were right there in the room with her. Automatically, she's inspired to use a calm, even-keeled voice. Once you're calm, you can move ahead to more effective ways of dealing with the situation.

The Save-the-Day Trap

Parents who fall into this habit try to do too much for their child. Well-intentioned and loving, they can't bear to see their child experience a disappointment or a bump in the road. They pay the fines for lost library books, rush forgotten milk money to school, buy new toys to replace those left in the rain and ruined. They give in to big-eyed pleadings for checkout lane balloons because they hate to spoil a lovely outing. They look the other way when requests to pick up books or tie a shoelace go ignored.

It can be hard to define where pure parental responsibility ends and a child's fledgling sense of responsibility begins. Certainly young children need lots of help. But as they approach the school years, they are ready to learn the consequences of their actions. And sometimes that includes unfortunate consequences, like broken toys or lunches sans milk. If you do everything for your child and spare her such inconveniences, she'll have smooth sailing, but only for the moment. She won't learn long-term lessons from the experience. Failure is not always a negative thing.

What works better: Set your child up for success by coaching him in what's expected or by issuing reminders. "It looks like it's going to rain. Have you brought your game inside? It will get ruined if it's left out." Then let him decide what happens next.

The Losing-It Trap

Parents who fall into this habit skip right past such time-consuming behavior modifiers as redirection or time-out. They ignore a simmering situation until it—and they—boil over. Or they are stressed, tired, or sick and snap at

HOW TO
Break a Power Struggle

Virtually any situation can escalate out of hand. You want your child to do one thing, but your child wants to do something else. Often you're in the middle of a power struggle before you realize it. If you give in, you feel as if you're backing down. And the firmer you dig in, the more deeply your child does the same. Power struggles peak with toddlers and preschoolers, who are determined to have their way at almost any cost.

Provided that your child isn't in any danger, the best thing to do is to *step back*. Look for an alternate route to achieving your aim. Shift the focus of the struggle. If, for example, your child has grabbed a fragile glass that means a great deal to you and refuses to relinquish it, stop demanding it. Instead, ask if she would like to have a sip of water out of the glass. Intrigued, she'll probably hand it over. Follow through and let her have a sip while you hold the glass. Then use the experience as a bridge to a related activity, such as asking her if she'd like to have some juice. Put the fragile glass away without comment and pour the juice into her usual cup. If she howls? At least the glass is safe, and you can explain that it's a special glass that's very delicate.

Sometimes changing your tone can break the impasse. Rather than continuing in a tense, angry voice, switch to a quieter, calm one.

Often a child stuck in a face-off grows increasingly defiant. Or she may lose control, crying or shouting as she feels backed into a corner. Whatever you do, don't punish her for fussing. That will only make the situation all the more explosive. Your child hasn't consciously instigated a power struggle as a particularly wicked way to get your goat. She simply wants something, or wants to do something. Keep the focus on the action, not the child.

the very first transgression. Basically, parents who lose it lack patience.

Yet all parents lose it, sometimes. Children can be exasperating. Schedules can be overly hectic. It happens. The occasional firestorm may shock or even frighten your child—and will probably produce the same reaction in you. But you'll both recover quickly. The trick is not to let explosions become regular events. If a sharp rebuke is your automatic first response to every little problem, your child is not likely to learn from his mistakes. Instead, he's liable to get sneaky and confine misdeeds to times and places when you're not looking in order to escape your wrath. An overblown reaction to a little error also robs you of the ability to make an impact when something goes seriously amiss.

HOW TO
Inspire Action in a Child Who's Dragging Her Feet

Kids are notorious about dragging their feet. When faced with a parental request, a child is apt to become the tortoise, not the hare. One tactic for getting them moving is to count to ten. Calmly give your child a warning, including a description of the consequence that will occur if the child fails to follow through: "You have until the count of ten to come to the bathroom for your bath, or you will have to go to bed without any bath or bedtime snack." Then start counting. Chances are good that the seriousness—and the challenge—of the countdown will produce results. If it doesn't, however, and you reach ten, move on to the consequences. Don't count to ten a second time or launch into a scolding.

What works better: On balance, discipline should involve far more acts of patience than punishment. If you find yourself resorting to yells and slaps every day, try to find a peaceful moment to step back and take a hard look at yourself. Are you stressed out by too many demands in your day? Look for ways to lighten your load, especially in the mornings and evenings, which tend to be most stressful for busy families. Taking care of young children is especially tiresome. Would it help to make more time to talk to other parents in your shoes? To hire a babysitter a few hours a week? To reexamine the way you and your partner share childcare? If you feel you chronically lose control because of something in your background (an abusive parent, for example) or your current lifestyle (such as pressure at work), consider talking to a counselor or therapist. A professional can help you figure out more constructive ways to handle your problem. Don't just do it for yourself—do it for your child.

CHAPTER SIX

The Problem Solver

The general principles of healthy discipline in this book can be applied to any situation. The behavior problems in this chapter have been singled out because they are especially common among young children. You'll find guidance on such behaviors as back talking, biting, clinginess, finicky eating, hitting, interrupting, and refusing to share.

The sections on one of the most unavoidable behaviors—tantrums—discuss the various forms of this problem and tell you the types of situations that tend to set them off.

Back Talk

Why it happens: You make a simple request. Your child will have none of it. He tosses down the gauntlet: "No!" "I don't want to!" "Make me!" Back talk is a form of defiance, a way to test your authority. It begins in toddlerhood, soon after your baby learns to speak, and persists in various permutations right on through adolescence. For young children, back talk is a shorthand way of saying, "Look, I've had enough." The child may be tired, or tired of having to answer to your directions. Back talk is a bid for independence.

What you can do: With toddlers and young preschoolers, you can't eliminate all negativism—but remember, it's just a stage. Use diversion or some focused one-on-one time to channel your child away from defiance and toward compliance.

For the preschool years on up, while it's commendable that your growing child is asserting her personhood, rudeness is still rudeness. Don't condone back talk. Instead, respond in a calm way: "Please don't talk that way. You sound mad—is there something you want to talk about?" The chance to unburden himself may come as a relief. Help your child learn more effective ways to express displeasure. Coach him, for instance, in using such phrases as, "I'm mad because . . ." or "I have a different idea." Even, "I don't want to because . . ." is an improvement.

Remember this: Children may unconsciously be patterning their negativism after you. When you're within earshot of your child, resist the temptation to make smart remarks at TV characters or about say, other drivers on the road with you, or in conversation. Also be aware that kids who hear the word *no* a lot tend to be kids who use that word often.

Bedtime Balking

Why it happens: Kids have a hard time going to bed for many reasons. They may be having too much fun being awake—being with you—to be inclined to stop. They may simply have trouble making transitions. And by the time your child is in preschool, she realizes that the whole world doesn't fall asleep when she does. She knows that you are still awake in another room, and wants to stay where the action is. Some children have trouble going to bed because they have inconsistent bedtime routines: A sleep habit has never been well established for them.

What you can do: Half the battle is setting up the idea that bedtime is not negotiable. Start by taking steps to make the road to Slumberland as peaceful and predictable as possible. Enforce a regular bedtime. A young child may not know when eight o'clock is, but can learn through having a regular routine that bedtime comes after taking a bath, putting on pajamas, and reading two books with Dad. Start to calm things down a half-hour or so before the bedtime ritual begins. That means no wild play or overly physical games. Switch to soothing activities, such as a milk-and-cracker snack.

Keep bedtime rituals to under an hour; fifteen to thirty minutes is ideal. Rule of thumb: If your routine is so elaborate that you'd have to write it all down for a babysitter, you're trying too hard. If your child tries to lure you into extensions—insisting, say, that you say good night to each and every stuffed animal, and adding new objects to the list night after night—put your foot down. Say, "You have too many animals for me to kiss each one good night. Let's pick three of them and then I'll blow one big kiss to all the rest."

Nip endless callbacks in the bud by asking your child before you leave the room if she needs anything else. "Do you want a glass of water? Do you need to use the potty?" If you've let the cascade of callbacks begin, it can be hard to disengage. Try using a gate on the door of a younger child to train her to stay in her room. Unfortunately, this approach will only work until she learns to climb over it. Once that happens you should calmly and matter-of-factly continue to lead your child back to bed. Don't make a fuss or start to scold; it's your attention that she seeks. Be consistent. If you give in and let your little pajamaed one stay up and snuggle with you on the sofa one night, you'll only exacerbate the problem. She'll want to do the same thing every night.

Remember this: If your child has a sudden change of heart about bedtime, try to pinpoint why. Some preschoolers go through a normal stage of fears associated with bedtime, for example. They may develop a fear of the dark, or believe that monsters have taken up residence under the bed. Take such fears seriously. Reassure your child that there's nothing to worry about. Offer comfort within reason. For example, install a night light in your child's room or let her sleep with the door open, but don't start a bad habit such as leaving the overhead light on or allowing your child to sleep in your bed (unless you are comfortable with the idea of sleeping together, a whole other issue, the consequences of which must be considered carefully by both parents). Times of stress or illness can interrupt formerly good sleep habits as well. It's smart to make exceptions for your child at such times.

Biting

Why it happens: Sinking one's teeth into a playmate's arm is horrifying to a parent, but is a common, normal behavior in a young child. Why a child bites is somewhat dependent on his age. Babies under about eight months of age bite because their teeth are just coming in. They usually bite while breast-feeding. Chomping down is a new sensation—another form of the oral explorations that all babies make. It may also help reduce the pain of teething. Older babies (eight to twelve months of age) bite playfully when they are excited; it's not intentional. Biting peaks in toddlerhood, as a way to vent feelings of frustration, jealousy, or anger in the absence of a vocabulary that could accomplish the same thing. Toddlers also lack the motor skills that would allow them to do many of the things they'd like to, which fuels frustration. It doesn't usually cross a toddler's mind that he's hurting someone when he bites. Biting usually ebbs by age 3. That's when language and motor skills improve.

If it persists after three, it tends to be done as a defense mechanism because the child feels physically threatened. It may also be an expression of stress, such as if the child is not receiving enough individualized attention or spends too many hours away from his parents. Or an ingrained biting habit may result from a child learning that it's an effective way to garner attention.

What you can do: Just because biting is developmentally normal doesn't mean you should condone it. This behavior needs to be nipped in the bud, as it were, before it becomes a bad habit. The kind of response you give determines whether the biting will persist. So *never overreact.* (This is hard if you are the one who has just been bitten, but a loud shriek will only delight the biter, who hadn't expected to elicit such a noise from you.) Calmly take the perpetrator aside, immediately, and look him in the eye. Say, "No biting." Don't laugh, get angry, or make a fuss. Since for the first bite or two, your child is simply learning what's appropriate or not, it isn't necessary to do anything more. A three-year-old who bites, on the other hand, might benefit from a brief time-out along with your reprimand.

Remember this: Sometimes children learn biting from their peers. A rash of biting incidents sometimes occurs in a playgroup or a day care situation. Often the children are just experimenting with something new they've learned. Biting in groups may also break out because the space is too small. Or there may not be enough toys, particularly multiple versions of the same plaything, for little ones who are not ready to share. Biting may be a symptom that a child is not yet ready for group play and would do better with one-on-one play dates. Even so, biting should be handled the same way each time, with calm reprimands. Don't reinforce the biting with attention; the parents' or teacher's attention should be directed to the child who has been bitten, while the biter goes ignored after being reprimanded.

Here's one way *not* to model behavior: Never bite a child back to show her what it feels like. It's best to not even nibble your child's arm or toes in play. Some experts believe that for chronic biters, parents should also eliminate roughhousing play, which can work the child up into an excited frenzy, making them unable to control the impulse to nip.

Bossiness

Why it happens: Normal development plays a role; so does habit. During toddlerhood, bossy behaviors are common among one- and two-year-olds. For example, your child may insist that only one specific person can sit in a certain chair—and woe to the visitor who tries to take a seat where Dad usually rests. The child may attempt to redirect the seating ("No! You sit here!") or even physically push the person out of the "wrong" chair. Toddlers are struggling to figure out the world. Once they understand a certain routine or sequence of events, it can be hard for them to see things a different way. "I want the pink cup," your child may demand, because she's drunk from the pink cup for the past two days straight. Order brings security. It's as if they want to will things to be just as they expect them to be.

Bossy tendencies may also crop up because young children are also continually being told what to do by those who are older. ("Let's use the potty." "Time to go home now." "Pick up your toy.") So in part, they are merely imitating what they see. Giving the orders themselves can also be an experiment—doing so provides a power surge that just feels good. Left unchecked, imperiousness can quickly change from cute quirk to tiresome bad habit.

What you can do: A certain amount of bossy behavior needs to be written off as part of growing up. A toddler truly can't understand, for example, why Grandma should be able to sit in the chair she's come to consider Daddy's chair, because her father normally sits there. A toddler is struggling mightily to make sense of the world, to make order out of chaos.

You can work with your child, however, to help him express his wishes in a civil fashion. Teach the concept of an "inside voice" and an "outside voice." Demonstrate for your child the difference between a whisper, a normal tone, and shouting. Explain which tones are acceptable for making requests. When tiny commands get physical, you may need to pick your child up and remove her from whatever (or whomever) she is pushing or hitting.

Take care not to give in to commands, even in fun. You're a parent, not an order taker. Insist on your child saying please or rephrasing a desire as a request, rather than as an order.

Explain to a preschooler that friends do not like to be ordered around. Model or role play the different ways your child might direct play with friends, or make suggestions about what to do.

Remember this: Some children are naturally more demanding and verbal than others. You can redirect the manner in which such a child expresses himself, but you can't change her assertive nature. Expect to hear many more suggestions, strong opinions, and instructions from this sort of child as she grows.

Clinging

Why it happens: A little shadow who follows close at Mom's or Dad's heels or who hides behind skirts and pant legs may have a naturally reserved personality. To venture into public is to step outside her secure, predictable world. This can make a shy child panicky. Another common reason for clinginess is that the child doesn't feel she's logging enough time with the parent. Perhaps they've been separated for long hours by work and day care. Or one of the parents has returned from a lengthy trip. When they're together again, the child doesn't want to let the parent out of her sight—in part because she simply misses the parent and wants to soak up togetherness, and in part because she's half afraid that if she occupies herself elsewhere, the parent might slip away again.

What you can do: Reserved or slow-to-warm-up children need time. Avoid throwing such a child into a series of new experiences. That's not to say you should shelter him from any outside encounters. Rather, look for ways of doing new things that build confidence. Attending nursery school just one or two days a week, for example, can be traumatic for such a child because she's unable to establish a regular routine. Each time she goes, it feels to her like beginning anew. Better to not attend at all, or to attend for a few hours four or five days a week, to establish a more predictable routine. Don't peel such a child off your leg and urge her to "Go on, have fun." You need to be more subtle. Help the child get engaged with a toy, in an activity, or point out an interesting sight. Take time to play with her, gradually stepping back. She needs extra time to adjust. If you must separate, as at day care, always say good-bye. It may induce tears and more clinging, but in the long run it's better than just sneaking off. Simply disappearing will only feed your child's insecurity, because she'll grow afraid that she'll never know whether you're going to be around unless she's hanging onto you.

Clinginess that's born of long separations is almost tougher, because you may not be able to adjust your schedule. Still, rearranging your time is worth considering. Excessive clinging can be a message to a parent that says, "I wish I could see you more." Make the most of the time you do spend together. Obviously, you can't devote every second to your child, but when you are playing together, give her your full attention. Generally, a child who feels secure and attached to a parent is better able to weather separations. Predictable routines, lots of positive reinforcement, and general closeness all help feed this sense of security.

Remember this: A certain amount of separation anxiety is normal in babies. It usually begins around six to nine months of age, becoming most intense around ten to eighteen months, and waning by age 2, although it can linger to age 3. Some kids don't seem to be bothered by it while others get quite panicky.

Dawdling

Why it happens: Adults are ruled by the clock. We have to be at work on time, get the kids to school at the designated hour, and show up when expected for doctor's appointments, meetings, sports games, and lessons.

Movies and radio news programs begin at specific times. We follow schedules, kept in our heads or in handy black notebooks. We're never more than a few feet from a clock, whether it's hanging on the wall, stuck to our wrist, or sitting in the small corner of our computer screen. "Don't be late," we say. "Hurry up."

Now imagine being free from all that. That's what life is like for your child. Even once she learns to tell time by age 6 or 7, it's a version of time with lots of rough edges, and lots of wiggle room for diversions. Young kids live in the here and now, clocks be darned.

What you can do: Verbally rushing your child tends to build his anxiety (as well as your own), usually resulting in a slow-down rather than a speed up. Actions usually speak louder than words. Rather than hectoring your child to "Hurry, hurry," you may need to lead her along. If you are late getting out the door, firmly help her with her socks, her shoes, and her coat. Don't stew about it, just do it.

Some children respond to games and incentives. You might challenge a poky pup at bedtime—can he put on his pajamas before you count to twenty? If you're taking a walk together and getting tired of stopping every five feet to examine a pebble or a stick, try picking up the pace by saying, "I'll race you to the next mailbox." Let your child know that if she eats breakfast and gets dressed promptly, she'll be able to play with a coveted toy a little longer before it's time to go to school.

Remember this: Keeping your child on a predictable schedule will help her develop a sense of time. You can use the mileposts of your day to let her know when other activities will take place. "After breakfast we are going to the library." "When I pick you up from school, we can play with your dollhouse." Praise your child not just for the things she does, but for performing them efficiently: "I liked it when you tied your shoes so quickly today."

Finicky Eater

Why it happens: Hassles over food usually start harmlessly. After the incredible growth rate of the first two years of life, toddler growth slows down a bit. Two-year-olds sometimes seem like they live on air because they eat so little. In fact, most young children choose a perfectly adequate diet for themselves over the course of a week. Children's portion sizes are smaller than adults', too. So what may seem like eating nothing to you is often quite adequate for your child. Individual children like different things as well. If your child declares that he doesn't like hamburger, he may simply not like the taste of it.

Problems develop when parents make an issue out of food. Most experts advise against forcing a child to eat anything. Food isn't worth a power struggle (which is what will inevitably result). Research suggests that coercive feeding practices can lead to weight problems or eating disorders later in life. The child learns to associate food with control.

What you can do: Present a healthful variety of foods and let your child decide what he wants to eat, and how much. Let his choices pass without comment. Don't cajole your child to join the "clean plate club" or to think about the poor starving children in some foreign land. Don't withhold dessert if your child has made a reasonable effort at sampling the main fare.

What should you do if your child takes one look at the stew you've lovingly prepared and says, "Yuck! I want fish sticks!" Don't fall into the habit of becoming a short-order cook. Make it a rule that if your child doesn't like what's being served for dinner, he can have a predetermined simple-to-fix alternative, such as a sandwich or a bowl of cereal. (Kids five and up should be able to prepare the alternative themselves.) If he chooses nothing but sandwiches for a month straight, fine. If you know that there are some foods your child balks at, you might present the meal as a choice: "Do you want stew or fish sticks?"

Remember this: Food battles are the most common and most unnecessary source of friction between parents and young children. Have regular mealtimes and snacktimes. Offer a balanced diet.

WHAT IF...

We're at a friend's house and our child refuses all the food that's being served. Finally the host offers some yogurt, which our child accepts, opens, and pronounces "Yucky"?

Tell your child, "Well, you chose it, so that's what you were served." Ask the host not to offer anything else, since she's gone out of her way already. While battles over food aren't worth the fuss, neither do you want to create a monster. Your job is to present the options and your child's job is to decide. Even if he has nothing to eat at all, he won't starve, and he can make up the calories at the next meal.

Don't let your child fill up on empty calories (potato chips, ice cream) if he doesn't also eat more nourishing fare. But beyond that, let your child be responsible for what goes in his stomach. Your main concern should be that your child is growing adequately, which your doctor can confirm at well-child checkups.

Greedy Gimmes

Why it happens: Kids typically launch into "I want" mode when they're overstimulated with temptations. The usual scene of such crimes: the grocery checkout lane, a toy store, pre-holiday shopping trips.

What you can do: To nip the gimmes in the bud, rehearse the outing ahead of time. Say, "Who's party is it? Joe's. So we're buying a toy for Joe. I can't buy two toys. And if you cry for a toy, what will I do? I'll remind you that I can only buy one toy. And if you still cry, what will we do? We will have to leave. Do you think you can help me pick a toy for Joe?" This approach acknowledges the difficulty of behaving well and challenges the child to show that he can do it. It also takes away the element of surprise. If your child does cry, whine, or otherwise beg for a toy of his own, you can remind him of your conversation. Don't be cross or judgmental.

If your child holds up well in the face of the challenge, you might consider offering a small reward, such as a cookie or a duplicate of Joe's gift. But this should come as a surprise. If you dangle it as a possibility beforehand, it's a bribe, which is much less effective in the long run than spontaneous positive reinforcement.

Remember this: Sometimes the easiest thing is to avoid a potentially explosive gimme trap altogether. Consider having your kids stay with a neighbor or partner while you go holiday shopping, and then return the favor. Or try going online. Resist starting your child too early on the what-do-you-want-to-get-for-Joe routine. If given the choice, of course your child will want to come to the toy store to select something. Purchase birthday presents for other children when your own child is not around. Before age 5, kids don't usually have too much vested interest in the gift they're giving. They care more about the treat bag they'll take home from the party.

Hitting

Why it happens: Kids resort to their fists for all the same reasons that grown-ups sometimes feel like punching someone out. Fury. Disappointment. Jealousy. Provocation. The difference, of course, is that grown-ups have learned how to exercise self-control. A child of any age can hit, but the behavior is especially common in toddlers and preschoolers, who lack more effective outlets for their emotions. New older siblings often poke and pinch their baby brother or sister in a bid for some of the attention they see the infant receiving.

What you can do: Hitting should never be condoned. Intervene swiftly. Remind your child of the no-hit rule and issue a consequence, such as a time-out. Be very clear about why, and enforce the rule consistently. Before carrying out the punishment, talk about what prompted the slug: "What made you mad?" Be empathetic, but don't get talked out of carrying out the penalty. Remind your child to use his words, rather than his fists: "Hitting hurts people and doesn't solve the real problem." Some parents tell their child to hit a pillow instead as a way to get the anger out. (See "Sibling Bickering," page 116.)

Remember this: Your goal is to teach your child self-control, so that the next time he feels like giving someone a wallop, he can find his own alternative way to vent his anger. That's why getting at the reason for hitting is important, as is equipping your child with other, acceptable responses such as words.

Ignoring

Why it happens: Kids ignore their parents because they want to. It's one teeny tiny way for them to exert a modicum of control over their lives. Parents often misread ignoring as deliberate disobedience. But the cause is usually something milder. The child is engrossed in an activity. He's having fun. Or perhaps he knows perfectly well why you want his presence—he's made a mess, done something wrong, or isn't ready to take a bath or go to bed. He's just wishing you away. A toddler will rationalize that if he can't see you, then you—and the matter at hand—simply don't exist.

WHAT WE DO
"Defusing Our Aggressive Child"

Shelli Jones describes her son, Matthew, as "demanding in every way." Matthew, two, is also aggressive. "He throws things or hits when he's mad or he doesn't get what he wants," says Shelli, who lives in Philadelphia. "And when he wants something and I'm not in the room with him, he'll come in and say, 'Mamma!' and then hit me."

The hitting habit began shortly after Matthew turned one. Usually, his aggressive behavior happens suddenly. If his stepsisters won't let him play with them, he'll try a few times to take their toys or otherwise ingratiate himself into their play. If they continue to resist—pow! Shelli tells him, 'No, you may not hit. You may throw yourself on the floor, just don't hit other people." She tries to redirect his aggression toward an inanimate object. "I say, 'If you're mad, you can bang on the wall, the floor, or a pillow,' " she explains.

Shelli also tries preventative measures, such as diverting his attention before he explodes. Her other tips for dealing with an aggressive child:

- **Be especially consistent.** "Don't make threats like, 'It's OK this time, but if you do it again I'll send you to time-out.' It will only confuse your child."

- **Be empathetic.** "I'll say things like, 'I know you're mad, but you can't hit.' "

- **Explore the reasons behind the outbursts.** "Matthew's aggression could be because he feels he's not getting the attention he wants. He wants it to be 'Me, me, me!' When we're alone with him, he's calmer. It helps us to try to understand things from his point of view."

- **Don't forget your child's positive qualities.** "He's a determined little kid— extremely intelligent and responsible for a two-year-old. He takes out the trash and always wants to help. When he's not angry he's such a cutie and you can't resist him. It's important to keep the whole Matthew in perspective."

What you can do: Go over to your child, rather than calling for him from across the room. Kneel down to his level. Repeat your message in a low, even tone. You don't need to use a lot of words that will just be tuned out.

Remember this: Getting upset and yelling from a distance is far less likely to get results than if you physically place yourself in front of your child. Keep calm, even though it can be extremely irritating when he ignores you.

Interrupting

Why it happens: Chronic interrupters are usually excited, showing off, or bidding for attention. Some particularly verbal kids just like to hear themselves talk. If the child is accustomed to receiving vast amounts of his parents' undivided attention when he interrupts, and the behavior goes unchecked, it can escalate into a regular pattern for the child.

Interrupting escalates when kids feel their parents' attention is being diverted, such as by someone visiting. That's why kids act worse just when you're hoping to show off to your neighbor how adorable they are. (See "Telephone Interruptions," page 124.)

Q&A
Is It a Hearing Problem?

Most instances of a child ignoring her parents has nothing to do with her hearing acuity. Still, if you have lingering doubts, it's a good idea for a doctor to evaluate her. The problem could be a temporary deafness, caused by middle ear infection or a buildup of earwax. Signs of a hearing disability include:

- Delayed speech
- Speech impairments (slurring certain sounds)
- Not being startled by sounds (especially during infancy)
- Repeatedly saying "What?"
- Consistently not responding to you

What you can do: Explain that talking is like playing on a seesaw. You have to take turns going up and down. One person can't be up in the air the whole time or it wouldn't be very much fun for either party. Some kids have no idea what they're doing wrong. Define it for them: "Interrupting is asking me a question or telling me something when I'm talking to another person or working at my desk." If the child is interrupting a younger sibling, say something like, "You're very good at telling stories, but your brother is not going to learn how to do that himself if you don't let him have a turn at talking." If you're the one being interrupted, express your disapproval: "It's not nice to keep interrupting. If you need something, you should say, 'Excuse me.' " And if you're barraged with "excuse mes" every ten seconds? Try a diversion, along with a warning. "I am going to give you a cup of crackers to eat. Please eat them without interrupting us. If you can't stop interrupting, you will have to go to your room for some quiet time."

Remember this: Be sure that your expectations for your child are realistic. Young children can't wait an eternity for certain kinds of attention, especially things like needing help with the toilet or being fed. Also, take care not to be an interrupter yourself when listening to your child.

Lying

Why it happens: What sounds like lying to adult ears isn't necessarily so. Until around four years of age, a child isn't really capable of a lie. That's because to lie, one must understand the difference between truth and falsity, and be capable of deliberate deception. Little ones don't really understand these sophisticated concepts. Their whole world is a fanciful place. A young child can't, for instance, tell the difference between what's fact and fiction on television or in books. She may half believe that her stuffed animals are walking, talking friends. She may have imaginary playmates. Because imaginations soar, they often tell tall tales that seem plausible to them. Toddlers and preschoolers are also notorious for denying that they've done something, even when it's perfectly obvious that they did. Are they lying when they say, "It wasn't me"? Not exactly. A young child may wish he hadn't done something and, simply by wishing it so, can convince himself it didn't happen. Again, the line between what's real and what's fantasy is a blurry one.

What you can do: Keep your expectations realistic. By kindergarten, a child understands truth versus fiction. But the impulse to embellish and exaggerate is still strong. It's best to gently point out the truth, if useful. ("Well, there is blue writing on the wall and you have a blue crayon in your hand.")

If an older child is deliberately lying, try to get her to talk about why she wouldn't want to tell the truth. Is she afraid of repercussions? Is she ashamed because she knows what she did was wrong? Talk about why truth is important and how being honest makes a person feel good inside. Tell the story of young George Washington fessing up to chopping down the cherry tree as an example. Still, it's usually worth treading lightly in this area with kids under age 6 as they discover what truthfulness means.

Remember this: A young child's tall tales are a sign of a vivid imagination. That's something to be proud of.

Name Calling

Why it happens: Hearing your sweet child call her friend "A big fat poo-poo butt" can be mortifying. It's even worse if *you're* the big fat poo-poo butt. Preschoolers and older kids call names for the same reason they swear: The use of new, silly monikers is a thrill. At first, they're not meant to be hurtful; the names are bandied about in fun. Put a group of toddlers or preschoolers together and the pure silliness of the sounds will have them howling. But soon a child realizes that these words have power. He uses them when he's feeling angry or impatient. (Variation: Telling a parent, "You're mean!" or "I hate you!")

What you can do: Don't give the words any additional power by reacting. Laughing or expressing horror merely encourages the behavior. Instead, take your child aside and say, "I don't like those words. Please use people's real names. If you are mad at Sam because he kicked your ball away, you need to use other words to tell him that." Point out that names can hurt someone's feelings; ask your child how he might feel if someone made fun of him through a made-up name.

Respond in similar fashion if you are the target of the name calling, even though it's admittedly harder to keep your composure. Say, "I don't like name-calling. Please call me Dad." If the child is persistent, continue to keep your cool but put her in time-out. A neutral behavior-breaker like time-out helps the child understand that the behavior is socially unacceptable.

Praise a name-caller when you hear her sticking to real names. Also teach your child to tell other children that if she is called a name, she doesn't want to play with them. Withholding her attention will curb their name-calling faster than if she cries or otherwise reacts.

Skip the old practice of washing your child's mouth out with soap. It's potentially dangerous (your child may gag or choke), not to mention rather barbaric in light of more educational options.

Remember this: Kids are listening, even when they don't appear to be. Avoid calling your boss, your neighbor, or public figures names. It's also best not to call your child by negative nicknames or descriptions, such as "You little rascal," "Messy girl," or "My devil boy."

Refusing to Share

Why it happens: Sharing is tough. Toddlers and preschoolers are naturally egocentric. One way they exert their sense of self is to hold tight to their possessions. "Mine!" is nothing less than a declaration of independence. It means "Me!"

What you can do: Forget about expecting a toddler to share. She is developmentally too immature. Trying to teach her this skill is simply not worth the power struggle. When two toddlers are playing together, provide identical toys to reduce friction. Even so, turf battles are bound to result. So always supervise toddlers closely. Instead of insisting that they share, try distraction, engaging one of the children in another toy.

You can also introduce the notion of taking turns. If Bess grabs for Kate's toy, tell Bess, "It's Kate's turn to play with the toy. When she's finished, it will be your turn." Then tell Kate, "After you're done playing with the toy, please give it to Bess." Often the child will give up the toy within seconds. The difference: She now feels that it's her idea to relinquish the toy, as opposed to a demand having been forced on her. With older kids, tell them, "You need to figure out a way that you can take turns with the toy, or I will remove it from play." If the bickering continues, take the object of contention away. Before play begins, set up sharing rules. Examples: *If you put something down, it means that you are finished with it. You may not grab anything out of someone else's hands.*

Never automatically punish a child for refusing to share toys. This is a very difficult task for some children. Instead, help her to see that you respect the boundaries of her personal property. When there is more than one child in a family, each sibling should have certain toys that are his or hers alone. Before a play date, ask your child if she would like to put any of her special things away in a safe place. You can also ask her to select which toys she'd like to share with her friend that day.

Remember this: It helps to role-model sharing. This gets your child accustomed to the word. When Mom and Dad are reading different sections of the newspaper together, point out that you are sharing the paper. If you are eating French fries in a restaurant, offer one to your child and say, "Would you like to share my fries?"

Running into the Street

Why it happens: No matter how many times you warn a child about the dangers of the street, this information doesn't stay in the front of his mind. He's apt to be more focused on the ball that just rolled out there or the friend he sees on the other side.

What you can do: Don't expect a child under age 4 or 5 to be careful around streets. It's your responsibility to keep a constant eye on him. Issue reminders. Hold his hand as you approach the street or if you are walking along one. If your child does dart, look him in the eye and say very sternly, "No crossing the street without holding a grown-up's hand." Some parents who ordinarily oppose corporal punishment feel that this is the one good time to spank, in order to underscore the message. Whether this is effective is dubious. Some experts feel that a young child still may not understand why he was struck, and instead get the message that hitting is okay.

Remember this: Safety comes before any disciplinary concern. Keep your eye on a young child when he's near the street (or playing in the front yard) until you are absolutely certain he's old enough to play or walk unsupervised there (which is rarely before kindergarten). Even then, keep issuing reminders and address transgressions immediately.

Screaming

Why it happens: Screamers usually get started accidentally. One of the remarkable discoveries a toddler makes early on is the amazing power of his own voice. It can talk, it can sing. It can whisper, and *it can be very loud!* In fact, he doesn't need to say a single word to be heard—he can just yell! Of all the variations in tone and pitch that your child experiments with, it doesn't take long before he discovers that yelling elicits the most delightful (to him, anyway) response. Mom looks. Mom shushes. Mom gets agitated.

What you can do: Most flirtations with screaming don't last very long, but they're not much fun for you no matter how often they occur. Whatever you do, don't yell back. Instead, reply to your child in a voice that's more quiet and a little bit slower than usual. Say, "Can you talk in a quiet voice like me?" Then switch to an even softer tone: "Can you whisper like this?" By your demonstrating more effective ways to use her voice, she learns a new form of self-control (controlling her vocal cords). And she might just become infatuated with whispering. Remind your child that screaming hurts your ears. Congratulate her when she changes her own tone: "I like that voice much better." Help your child learn the difference between an acceptable indoor voice (normal tones) and an outdoor voice, which can be louder.

Remember this: Kids learn by example. If a parent relies on shouting or yelling when angry or upset, the child is more likely to experiment with screaming herself.

Sibling Bickering

Why it happens: Siblings fight for the same reason people climb mountains: Because they're there. Though that explanation may sound glib, it's accurate. Above all, a child wants his parents' complete, undivided attention—but so does his sibling. Therefore the very presence of the sibling can cause an undercurrent of irritation, which shows up in feuds over who sits where, which color cup each child is given, and who's playing with a given toy.

Rivalry tends to be most fierce when kids are close in age. Children born more than three years apart are generally more developmentally mature and more secure in their relationships with their parents. The older child who is three or more tends to feel less threatened by a newborn. As the pair grow, their interests are less likely to overlap than when siblings are closer in age, which also helps minimize feuds. That's not to say that kids spaced more than three years apart will never bicker; they surely will. But the squabbles are apt to be less intense.

What you can do: When a new sibling is born, look for ways to involve your child, such as retrieving diapers or reading a book together while you are breast-feeding. It can be challenging, since caring for a newborn is so time-consuming, but your older child will notice your efforts. You can't make the rivalry go away, but you can offer extra reassurances during the topsy-turvy first weeks.

WHAT WE DO
"How We Handle Sibling Rivalry"

The MacMahans have a motto in their house: "Nastiness is something that's just not tolerated." Christine encourages her sons, five-year-old Joey and three-year-old Justin, to be close. "Society has way too much competition. We stress lack of competition in the family and focus on the family working as a team. As long as you try your best, you're a winner," says the Huntersville, North Carolina, mother.

Still, as in any family with siblings close in age, there is squabbling. When the family reads books together, for example, the boys are quick to argue over who picks what to read. So Christine will ask, "What do we need to do?" And Joey and Justin will yell out, "Compromise!" Joey then chooses three books and Justin chooses which one of the three to read. They switch roles the next night. "It works because they both become part of the decision," Christine explains.

Competition between the boys started when Justin began crawling and discovered Joey's toys. Joey would hit Justin in defense and tensions would rise. Christine taught Joey distraction techniques to deal with those situations. Now, Joey will say to Justin, "Look at this other toy—this one's better."

No matter what the situation, the boys are taught to patch things up. "I'll tell one of my boys that he upset his brother and it's up to him to fix it," Christine says. A quick "Come help me cheer him up" always gets the ball rolling.

More of Christine's tips on handling sibling rivalry:

- **Allocate time alone.** "When they are bickering I'll say, 'Sounds like you need time apart to play alone.' They'll fight me on it, but they really need and appreciate it."

- **Empower your child.** "You need to show boundaries, but not get carried away by being too harsh. Showing your child how to be part of the solution will help him stay within your boundaries."

- **Your attitude sets the stage for behavior.** "If you want your children to get along, you need to expect that from them."

- **Love them every time you correct them.** "I start out by saying, 'I love you very much,' then I explain, 'This is why you can't do that.' "

If your children are older, find ways you can offer both of them your attention, one-on-one and together. Avoid putting one child on a pedestal, even if he's particularly talented or bright in a certain arena. Never compare siblings. It's best to find and praise their individual strengths and communicate the message that everyone is special in different ways.

Realize that a certain amount of fussing simply goes with the territory of having two or more children. Learn to ignore the petty bickering and save your energy for the big deals, such as episodes involving ugly behavior like hitting. Left alone, kids can learn to settle many disputes on their own. If you intervene too quickly, you deprive them of the opportunity to learn negotiation. You also risk encouraging tattling, as one child may fall into the habit of coming to you for help whenever his sibling so much as looks at him the wrong way. What's more, the complainer may have done something to provoke the other child first. Lay certain ground rules about how siblings are expected to behave toward one another, and follow through with consequences when those rules are broken.

Remember this: Whole books have been written on the subject of sibling rivalry. If you're especially frustrated, you certainly might pick up additional pointers by consulting them. But realize that there's no way you can completely eliminate the tendency. At best, you can hope to teach mutual love, tolerance, and respect.

Swearing

Why it happens: Children repeat everything they hear. That includes swear words. In fact, bad words hold special appeal to young kids for a number of reasons. First, because they are usually uttered with a certain amount of passion, a child senses intuitively that curse words are not part of everyday vocabulary, thus giving them a certain cachet. Second, such words inevitably get a rise out of grown-ups (whether a smirk or a scowl), which adds to their allure. The sound and meaning of the word has an appeal too. Two-year-olds merely like the alliterative ring of *doo-doo* and *ca-ca*. Many of the words preschoolers are attracted to involve bodily functions (poopie-head, butt, fart). For older children, the focus shifts to vaguely sexual words (penis-head, boobs). Youngsters use dirty words to show they're not afraid. Finally, kids use such language to draw attention to themselves. They don't always know, or care, about the meanings attached to such talk. It's the mere sound of the words that is funny or otherwise satisfying. If peers laugh, or are also using such words, that's all the incentive a peer-oriented kindergartener or first-grader needs.

What you can do: Young kids aren't even aware that a word they repeat is bad unless this is pointed out. But say so in a low-key way, lest you draw too much attention to the word, giving it too much value. ("We don't use that word.") Your child may not understand the word's meaning, or require an explanation from you. You can even ignore much of the preschool-set potty talk. Just don't laugh. A lot of this talk is hilarious coming from the mouths of babes, but smiling gives tacit approval and merely eggs a child on.

With kids five and up, however, it's wise to intervene. Make it clear that you don't condone obscene language. Keep your reactions to vulgarities consistent: Don't laugh today and scold tomorrow. Respond to repeat offenders with a time-out or by revoking privileges. Tell your child that many people are upset or offended to hear it. Explain why certain words are unacceptable. Use clinical terms for body parts (penis, vagina). Or teach more acceptable alternatives for common curses (heck, darn). Some parents restrict certain language to the outdoors.

If your child utters an oath because she's just smacked a plastic hammer on her hand, let her know that you disapprove of the language without denying her the accompanying emotion. Say something like, "I know it hurt when you hit your thumb. But I want you to use words like 'Ouch' or 'Darn' when that happens to express your anger. The word you said was not polite."

What if your child is clearly saying a word again and again in an effort to get your goat, say because the first time he did it, you let loose a strong reaction? Don't take the bait again. Practice selective ignoring. Eventually, seeing that the word has lost its impact, your child will probably abandon it.

Remember this: Cursing is everywhere in our culture. Even prime-time TV shows are rife with it. Realize that the majority of movies (even PG-rated ones) and family television programs will expose your child to inappropriate language. Think carefully about what you allow your child to watch and listen to. Resist the temptation to rush him into pop culture; that will happen soon enough. Pay attention to your own speech, too.

Taking Things

Why it happens: Preschool shoplifters have different ideas about ownership than do their parents. They haven't yet grasped the concept of "This is yours and this is mine." Nor do they fully appreciate the idea of paying for goods in a store as a precursor to ownership, no matter how many times they've witnessed you opening your wallet and forking over cash. What's more, social rules about ownership can be confusing. Your child is allowed to take a balloon home from a restaurant, for example, but not the balloons he sees in a store display. Why can't he bring home a toy car from his friend's house if he was able to bring home one of the neat pencils he admired in Dad's office? Greed or desire overwhelms all else: The child sees something, the child wants something, the child helps himself to it. This behavior changes around age 5, when a child more clearly comprehends the rules of ownership.

What you can do: If you catch your thief in the act, explain: "That candy bar belongs to the store, not to us." Or say, "This is Bryson's car. You can play with it at his house, but when we leave, it has to stay here." Skip the shaming lectures. Your child won't develop a sense of guilt or morality until the early grade-school years.

What if you find a toy in your child's pocket after you return home? Ask, in a nonaccusatory tone, where the object came from. Often the answer will be, "I don't know." Then you can say, "Well, it doesn't belong to us. Let's think about who else must be missing it." Remind your child how he felt when he couldn't find one of his favorite toys and point out that his friend probably feels the same way now. Tell him matter-of-factly that he can't keep it. "This ball belongs to the store. I know you really wished you could have it but we have to bring it back." Skip the scolding. You simply want your child to gain a rudimentary understanding of ownership. Stick to, "It's wrong to take what isn't ours."

Your child should accompany you when the toy is returned. Tell the clerk, "Josh wants you have this back. He didn't realize that it belongs to the store and not to him." It's helpful to call the store in advance, if feasible, so that the clerk can chime in with praise when the object is returned. Although you shouldn't punish, neither should you reward the child. Don't buy the ball when you return to the store or let him play with it.

Remember this: Even though a preschooler doesn't deliberately steal, don't let the incident slide. That would set a precedent that there was nothing wrong with what he did. Always return pilfered goods, with your tot in tow.

Tantrums

Why it happens: A temper tantrum usually rears its angry head as a result of frustration. It's an emotional meltdown caused when a child can't verbally express anger or disappointment and doesn't know a more effective way to react. Tantrums are utterly normal, and one part of growing up. Losing control is a child's way of saying, "Help! I'm emotionally overloaded!" Tantrum triggers tend to vary according to a child's age. From twelve months, when they first show up, to about eighteen months, kids hate to be confined, whether in a car seat, a playpen, or your arms. After age 2, toddlers begin to chafe at rules, such as not throwing food or having to take a nap. This pattern continues to age 3, as the child continues to want to exert his independence and finds it difficult to compromise or share. Tantrums usually subside by kindergarten, as the child learns more effective methods to express displeasure and achieve his own goals.

What you can do: Preventatively, you can tailor your response to the tantrum's cause. For example, don't keep a young child immobile too long. Alternate sedentary activities with more physical ones. Keep your expectations realistic, too. Want your two-year-old to play quietly in a corner while you host a cocktail party for fifty? Think again. Giving a child choices, within limits, and some sense that he can do as he likes, within reason, will go a long way toward stoking his budding independence. Generally, children who live in households with lots of routines and clearly defined limits tend to have fewer tantrums, because there are fewer surprises in their lives. Even so, some tantrums are simply unavoidable.

Some children are more prone to tantrums than others. A highly sensitive child has intense feelings. Ironically, such a child also tends to have a great sense of humor and be quite upbeat much of the time.

Like a volcanic eruption, the child will usually show some warning signs that he's about to blow. Puffs of smoke and ash include whining and resistance. When you sense a flare-up on the way, try changing the scene. If your child

CHECKLIST
Tantrum Triggers

You can avoid some tantrums by minimizing the situations that set a child off. These include:

✔ Extreme fatigue (skipped nap, late nights)

✔ Not getting what she wants fast enough

✔ Being unable to verbalize her desires

✔ Hunger

✔ Sickness

✔ Frustration from physical inability to do something (fine motor skills, learning to read)

✔ Having too much expected of her for her age or developmental stage

✔ Big life changes (new sibling, new sitter)

✔ Little life changes (popped balloon, time to leave playground)

✔ Loss of security object (blanket)

✔ Stressed schedule (too many errands, classes, play dates)

has just thrown a puzzle on the ground because he could not do it, going outside to run around may help him cool down. If your child can talk, ask, "Tell me what made you mad. It's hard when your block tower gets knocked over, isn't it?" If possible, give your child choices that feed her sense of self-control: "Do you want to have quiet time in your room or rest on this blanket while I fold laundry?" Disengaging from power struggles is another way to stop a balky child's digging in before it gets out of control.

Once the child's top has blown, however, there's usually little you can do to reverse the course. Stay nearby to keep an eye on your child, but go about your usual business. Don't reward the behavior with lavish attention. Many kids refuse to be held as they flail away. But keep your child (and yourself) from harm—don't allow kicking or head banging, for instance. Move her to a safer place, such as a carpet in place of a chair or a wood floor, or hold her tightly to avoid danger.

Otherwise, the best reaction is to let your child burn herself out. Once she's calm, follow up the episode with a little heart-to-heart talk: "I know you didn't want to stop playing because it was nap time. It's hard to leave one fun thing behind for something else. Why don't we read a few books together on your bed right now?" Use your judgment about having a recap speech with very young children, though. The mere mention of the trigger can crank things up all over again.

Remember this: Don't attempt to reason with a child in the throes of a temper tantrum. Not only do young children not respond to logical arguments, but in this particular situation your child is in no mood to listen to anything. Nor is it wise to capitulate, giving in to the desire that launched a power struggle in the first place. That will only teach your child that losing control is an excellent way to achieve his wants.

Tantrums in Public

Why it happens: Along with an increased number of the usual stresses that inspire tantrums (temptations, confinement, a battle of wills), flare-ups often occur in public because your child has an audience. The explosion becomes a grand attention-getting device as well as an unholy emotional release.

What you can do: First, disengage from what you sense others are thinking. The judgmental looks of passers-by can make you more critical of yourself and, in turn, of your child. Anyway, those staring onlookers are probably just feeling relief that they're not in your shoes. If they are parents, they've been there before. They're probably reminiscing, not thinking, "What a lousy mother!" Exit the scene if you prefer.

Sometimes a tantrum can be sidestepped by applying all the prevention tactics you can muster. Schedule outings for times when your child is fed and well rested. Keep her occupied. Let her find and fetch items at the store, sing songs together, or invent games like spotting different colors or shapes. Yes, it takes energy. But it's a more constructive energy than you'd use mopping up a meltdown.

If the explosion threatens anyway, remind your child what will happen if she can't keep her cool. Say something like, "I think we need to take a break, so you can sit here with me. We'll count to ten. Then you can continue helping me. But if you can't do that, we'll just go back to the car." It's not a threat. Sound matter-of-fact and calm. It may be that your child is at the end of her rope and can't contain herself. In that event, you just need to leave. Inconvenient, to be sure, but it sends the message that you won't tolerate outrageous behavior, and at the same time it's respectful of your child's limits.

Tantrums often occur when it's time to leave someplace but your child isn't ready, such as the playground, a store that has a train table or other playthings on display. Help make transitions smoother by initiating a good-bye ritual. Help the child wind down with a methodical farewell to friends, the sandbox, the tank engine, and so on. And if the child still blows up? Be empathetic. Tell her, "I know it's too bad that we have to go just when you were having such a wonderful time." Then just pick her up and go.

Remember this: Two- and three-year-old children are tantrum-prone. If possible, take some of the pressure off your child by minimizing morning rushes and other running around. Reexamine your expectations. A little boy in a restaurant with neatly combed hair and his Mister Rogers cardigan may look grown-up, but inside he's still your two-year-old. Just because he's dressed up doesn't mean he's ready to sit through a five-course meal.

Telephone Interruptions

Why it happens: Talking on the phone is a megawatt announcement to your child that he is not at center court in your attentions. Never mind that he was happily playing by himself just before you dialed and didn't seem the least bit interested in you. That was then. This is now.

What you can do: Try some preventative measures. Let your child know that you are going to be on the phone. Instruct him that if he needs you, he should interrupt you with a polite "Excuse me." Forewarn that you will not respond to whining or shirt pulling. Some parents keep special colored markers, Play-Doh, or other treat in a special place to pull out when they need a bit of privacy to make a call. You might give a younger child a toy telephone to play with while you talk. When you're off the phone, you can practice having conversations together.

But be realistic. Don't expect to handle a thirty-minute business call with a little one around. Keep your conversation brief.

Remember this: Sometimes kids whine and interrupt because they really do crave your attention. Maybe your child is not feeling well. Or you've been separated all day at work and, even though he was playing alone before you began to talk on the phone, he's craving some connectedness. If you stop what you're doing and indulge the child even for a short while, he's more likely to allow you to go off later.

Touching Something Dangerous

Why it happens: Little ones are attracted to objects and places because they are interesting, colorful, new, or fun. They don't purposely single out electrical outlets, toilet bowls, and knives simply because such things are dangerous.

What you can do: Once your child is already into something, use distraction. Either remove the object or steer your child away, with a firm, "Not for baby." (Or, "Not for Adam.") Then immediately engage him in something equally alluring. Slapping the child's hand or lecturing him is pointless. All he was doing was playing.

Remember this: Childproofing is your best defense against young explorers. Aside from the usual steps—installing outlet plugs, using gates at dangerous stairways, turning pot handles inward, and so on—you may want to take extra steps if your child seems drawn to particular hazards. For example, if he can't stay away from the toilet bowl, it may not be enough to keep the door closed and the lid down. You may also want to install toilet locks.

TV Addiction

Why it happens: Television is seductive. It's bright and colorful entertainment, easy to sit back and take in. Young children who tune in to regular programs may enjoy the social aspect of TV; to watch is to commune with her familiar friends Dipsy, Arthur, Little Bill, Madeline, and Big Bird. There's nothing inherently wrong with viewing age-appropriate programming in reasonable doses. TV addiction—defined as begging to watch more television than the parent thinks is optimal—happens because parents let it happen.

What you can do: Set house rules, then stick to them. Examples: Only two hours of TV a day. Or no TV before school. Or no TV until homework is finished. Or one half-hour video is allowed before bedtime. Kids are less apt to resist limitations on TV viewing when the rules have become part of an expected routine.

Remember this: Some studies have found an association between excessive TV viewing and increased violence and obesity in children. It has been claimed that overreliance on TV stunts creativity and social skills. How much is too much, however, is open to debate. For some families, an hour a day is plenty. Others are more permissive. You need to consider the whole of your child's day in deciding how much TV he should be allowed to watch. Does he engage in other activities, including a healthy amount of outdoor play? An equally important consideration is what your child is watching. There have never been more good programming options for young children, and

Q&A

What About Computers?

The advice about TV addiction also holds perfectly true for use of computers and electronic games. There is no hard-and-fast rule about how much is too much. Every family must decide its own house rules regarding kids and computers. Considering that children are being introduced to a mouse younger than ever, it's never too early to establish your own viewpoint about limits.

Remember that although a computer is slightly more interactive than a TV set, both activities are generally passive. They involve sitting still and looking at a screen. Don't be misled into thinking that computer time is necessarily better for your child than TV viewing. As with TV, consider your child's overall day and balance of activities. Count all kinds of screen-time together: two hours of TV and two hours of computer games a day still add up to four hours of sitting around.

Also be aware that many early-education experts frown on the idea of computer use for infants and toddlers, despite the prevalence of software aimed at these age groups. Young children learn best through interactive, tactile play. They need to touch and mouth their playthings. Computers are not even considered essential experience for preschoolers; they're a fun extra. Keep sessions brief—thirty to forty-five minutes at a time is plenty. Don't worry that your little one will be somehow left in the dust if he doesn't log on until he's of school age. There's no chance that a child born at the turn of the century will somehow escape computer literacy. It's less a skill to learn these days than a fact of life.

the pervasiveness of VCR and quality videotapes means that you can bypass the channel surfing altogether.

Whining

Why it happens: That sound—it's one of screeching or moaning, like a siren that never leaves your street or a mosquito stuck in your left ear. All kids whine—until they're taught other alternatives. Whining is a natural step between crying and learning to talk. Needy toddlers rely on the same plaintive sound they used as babies, with a few words mixed in, to signal their wants and needs. Because they are small and powerless, their lack of control over the world gives them plenty to whine about. Toddlers and preschoolers also have a primitive sense of time. When they want something, they want it *now*. "In five minutes" carries little meaning. Whining escalates when kids are tired, hungry, or sick.

Kids whine because it works. Parents give in to whining because the annoying sound stops. But kids then continue the behavior because they see that it works. Both the parent's and the child's behavior reinforce one another.

Whining persists when it's left unchecked. Children also tend to use it when parents put them off a lot: "We'll do it later." "After dinner you can have the cake." "In a minute, okay?" It doesn't matter if you've simply forgotten, or been distracted. The result is that the child is told one thing, but something else happens. Whining becomes habitual because the child learns that if he doesn't persist now, the promise may never be realized. By the same token, a child who knows that promises will be followed through develops trust and the ability to wait patiently.

What you can do: Label the behavior for your child so she understands what whining is in the first place. Say something like, "What's that? I hear whining. As soon as you can talk calmly like a big girl, I'll get it for you." Remain matter-of-fact. For very young toddlers, simplify this to: "You want juice now? Can you say 'Juice, please,' in a nice way?" Demonstrate what a nice tone sounds like. Once your child understands what whining is and why it's not acceptable, you can advance to ignoring the behavior. Warn your child only once. The more you say things like, "I won't speak to you until you stop," or "If you don't stop that noise you'll be in trouble," the more your child is apt to persist, just to try to get a rise out of you. Be consistent in refusing to respond to a whine. If you give in today but not tomorrow, your child winds up continuing to whine because she feels that it's worth a shot.

Examine your own behavior. Are you unwittingly fueling whines by using a complaining tone yourself about work or laundry or your mother-in-law? Also ask yourself if you're continually putting your child off. On the one hand, you don't want to give in to whines, thus rewarding them. But sometimes kids have legitimate complaints because busy parents say, "Later, later," without following through. Or they eventually do pour the juice or help the child with her shoes, but far later than seems reasonable to a toddler or preschooler who still hasn't developed a good sense of time.

CHECKLIST
Best and Worst Whine-Stoppers

Responses That Don't Work:

✔ **Threats:** "Quit that or I'll really give you something to whine about!"

✔ **Commands:** "Stop it right now!"

✔ **Giving in:** "All right already. You can have the candy bar."

✔ **Making vague promises:** "Maybe later."

✔ **Promising but not following through:** "I'll be there in a second."

✔ **Immediate punishment:** "Enough! Time-out for you!"

✔ **Whining yourself:** "Pleeeze stop! Why do you have to whine all the time? It drives me craaazy!"

Responses That Do Work:

✔ **Redirecting:** "If you can say that in a normal voice, we can talk about it."

✔ **Ignoring:** "I don't pay attention to whines." (Or say nothing.)

✔ **Humor:** "Excuse me? I can't understand Whinese."

✔ **Labeling the whine:** "That's a whine, not a nice way to ask for something. Here's a better way to say it." (And model the proper tone.)

✔ **Praising:** "I like how you asked me that. You're much more fun to be around when you're not making that sound."

✔ **Empathy:** "You sound very unhappy. Why don't you sit there and think about why you're sad, and when you're calmer, I can help you."

✔ **Admiring good behavior:** "I haven't heard you whine all day and that makes me happy. Let's go outside."

Remember this: Some kids whine more in public. They know that making a scene puts you on the spot. Don't succumb. If you're heading into a whine-prone situation—say, a toy store loaded with "gimme" temptations—warn your child in advance what's expected of him. "I am not here to buy you a toy today, but you can look and play with the display toys. But if you start to whine, we will have to leave." Generally, you should treat whining in public no differently from whining at home.

Index